THE HISTORY
OF
WESTERN
ETHICS

THE BRITANNICA GUIDE TO ETHICS

THE HISTORY
OF
WESTERN
ETHICS

EDITED BY BRIAN DUIGNAN, SENIOR EDITOR, PHILOSOPHY AND RELIGION

Published in 2011 by Britannica Educational Publishing
(a trademark of Encyclopædia Britannica, Inc.)
in association with Rosen Educational Services, LLC
29 East 21st Street, New York, NY 10010.

Distributed exclusively by Rosen Educational Services.
For a listing of additional Britannica Educational Publishing titles, call toll free (800) 237-9932.

First Edition

Britannica Educational Publishing
Michael I. Levy: Executive Editor
J.E. Luebering: Senior Manager
Marilyn L. Barton: Senior Coordinator, Production Control
Steven Bosco: Director, Editorial Technologies
Lisa S. Braucher: Senior Producer and Data Editor
Yvette Charboneau: Senior Copy Editor
Kathy Nakamura: Manager, Media Acquisition
Brian Duignan: Senior Editor, Philosophy and Religion

Rosen Educational Services
Heather M. Moore Niver: Editor
Nicholas Croce: Editor
Nelson Sá: Art Director
Cindy Reiman: Photography Manager
Nicole Russo: Designer
Matthew Cauli: Cover Design
Introduction by Brian Duignan

Library of Congress Cataloging-in-Publication Data

The History of Western Ethics / edited by Brian Duignan. -- 1st ed.
    p. cm. — (The Britannica Guide to Ethics)
"In association with Britannica Educational Publishing, Rosen Educational Services."
Includes bibliographical references and index.
ISBN 978-1-61530-301-4 (library binding)
1. Ethics—History. I. Duignan, Brian.
BJ71.H563 2011
170.9—dc22

                                                          2010014726

Manufactured in the United States of America

Cover Photo: Imagno/Hulton Archive/Getty Images

CONTENTS

10

46

61

INTRODUCTION

Each year thousands of babies are born with Down syndrome, a congenital (genetic) disorder that typically results in mild to severe intellectual disability (mental retardation), physical deformities of the face and head, and malformations of the heart and kidneys. In some cases the heart or kidney defects are life threatening and cannot be corrected by surgery, and the baby dies soon after birth. People with Down syndrome typically have much shorter life expectancies than normal adults, and those in which the syndrome is severe are never able to care for themselves. Through diagnostic tests it is now possible to detect the presence of Down syndrome in a fetus after about 11 weeks of pregnancy. On the basis of such information, some couples decide to abort a fetus with Down syndrome. In other cases, the parents allow the baby to die by withholding surgery that could correct a life-threatening defect.

Some people think that decisions like these are morally wrong. To abort the fetus, or to allow the baby to die, solely because it has Down syndrome, they may argue, is to assume that the life of a person with Down syndrome is less valuable than that of a healthy person, or that a person with Down syndrome somehow has lesser rights. Others think that these decisions, though tragic, are right, because they have the effect of sparing the fetus or baby with Down syndrome a lifetime of physical and emotional suffering. Still others — perhaps most of us, in fact — think it is just unclear what the morally right (or wrong) course of action is. We have conflicting moral intuitions, which pull us in different directions.

So what is the right thing to do?

It may be tempting to say that there is no correct answer to this question: different people have different

Aristotle and Plato are two of the strongest pillars of modern ethical thought. Hulton Archive/Getty Images

beliefs about what is right and wrong or good and bad, and there is no independent standard by which to judge between them—no standard that is valid for all people in all societies in all time periods. The most that one can say about the present case, according to this view, is that aborting the fetus or allowing the baby to die is not absolutely right or wrong but only right for some couples or families and wrong for others.

Ethical relativism—the idea that morality is not absolute but relative to individuals, communities, or societies—has been a common view of morality for thousands of years. Some people are attracted to relativism because it seems to reflect their value of tolerance for other people's beliefs or cultural traditions. Others, it must be admitted, simply resign themselves to it, either because they believe that moral dilemmas are inherently mysterious or because they wish to save themselves the trouble of thinking through difficult cases. Whatever the reasons for its popular appeal, relativism has been a legitimate and powerful theoretical perspective within ethical philosophy since ancient times.

Ethics is the philosophical study of morality. It is importantly distinct from moral psychology, which is the empirical study of the ways in which people actually think about morality and what causes them to think as they do. Ethics, in contrast, is concerned with the content, or substance, of morality. It is typically divided into three fields: normative ethics, which formulates general standards for deciding what is right or wrong and good or bad; applied ethics, which (as the name implies) applies such standards to real-life moral problems, such as the one involving babies born with Down syndrome; and metaethics (sometimes called theoretical ethics), which addresses questions about the nature of moral concepts and moral judgments—for example, are moral judgments absolute or relative?

Western ethics was developed some 2,000 to 2,500 years ago by the ancient Greeks, who were also responsible for founding all the other major branches of Western philosophy: metaphysics (the study of the ultimate nature of reality), epistemology (the study of knowledge), and logic. As they did for the other branches, the Greeks provided most of the basic concepts and vocabulary, and some of the main problems and theories, of subsequent Western ethics.

Greek ethics characteristically conceived of morality in terms of the "good life" for human beings. For Aristotle (*c.* 384–322 BCE), the best life is one in which the individual exercises fully the capacity that distinguishes human beings from all other things: the capacity to reason. However, the contemplative life, to be fruitful and fulfilling, requires the possession of the entire range of moral virtues, such as practical wisdom and temperance. Virtuous activity is thus both a means toward, and an essential constituent of, a happy life, and Aristotle accordingly defines happiness as the "activity of reason in accordance with virtue." Aristotle's eudaemonism (from the Greek *eudaemonia*, "happiness"), as this kind of theory is called, was the foundation of the ethics of the medieval philosopher St. Thomas Aquinas (1225–74). Eudaemonism was revived (although not under that name) in the 20th century by philosophers who had come to regard the modern focus on the rightness or wrongness of actions as not properly reflective of the richness of human moral experience.

The Hellenistic philosopher Epicurus (341–270 BCE) articulated the view that the only good is pleasure and the only evil pain. Therefore, right actions are those that maximize the former or minimize the latter. Epicurus's ethics was the first systematic example of consequentialism, a class of normative-ethical theory according to which actions are right or wrong depending on the nature of their consequences. Epicureanism was also the forerunner of utilitarianism, a theory developed in the 18th century that held that right action is that which produces the greatest happiness for the greatest number of people. Utilitarianism, as formulated by Jeremy Bentham (1748–1832) and refined by John Stuart Mill (1806–73), became the ethical foundation of a broad movement of social reform in Britain, and it remained the dominant form of normative-ethical theory in that country until the early 20th century.

In the field of metaethics, the Greeks were the first to articulate and explore ethical relativism. The theory was defended in the 5th century BCE by the Sophists, a group of scholars who travelled throughout the Greek world teaching mainly forensics, or the art of logical argument, for money. Protagoras (c. 485–c. 410 BCE), for example, held that what is just in one community may be unjust in another, there being no way to decide which community is correct, and Thrasymachus (flourished late 5th century BCE) famously argued that justice is whatever is in the interests of the stronger. Thrasymachus's view is in fact perennial. It has appeared in various guises in the work of several modern and contemporary philosophers, including Niccolò Machiavelli (1469–1527), Friedrich Nietzsche (1844–1900), and the 20th-century postmodernists (discussed further in the text below).

It is in the field of metaethics that the Greek patrimony in Western ethics is most evident. Greek ethics was concerned with three metaethical problems, which can be expressed in the following questions: (1) Is morality objective or subjective, absolute or relative? (2) How is moral knowledge possible? (3) Why should I (or any other person) be moral?" The latter question is also expressed as "Is it in one's self-interest to be moral?" and "Is it rational to be moral?" These obviously related questions have been at the heart of metaethical theorizing ever since.

Plato (c. 428–c. 348 BCE), following his teacher Socrates (c. 470–399 BCE), held that virtue is a form of knowledge. For Plato, but not for Socrates, such knowledge is attained by grasping the "form" of the virtue in question—a perfect, unchanging, and eternal entity, imperfectly approximated in those who are said to possess it—and eventually the form of Virtue and ultimately that of the Good. The happy life belongs to the person who possesses the virtue of justice, which consists of a harmony between the rational, spiritual, and appetitive parts of the soul, each of which accordingly acts in keeping with the virtues appropriate to it. He who is just, therefore, necessarily possesses all the other virtues.

The possibility of moral knowledge (as well as every other kind) was questioned by Pyrrhon of Elis (360–272 BCE). According to the school established by his followers, Academic Skepticism, there are equally good reasons for affirming and denying any positive assertion, including moral ones. Although some Skeptics held that, because true knowledge is impossible, one must resign oneself to living in accord with "appearances" and local custom, they did not thereby endorse ethical relativism. After all, the claim that morality is relative is itself a positive assertion, which therefore cannot be known if the assumptions of Skepticism are correct.

Although medieval philosophers were not much concerned with skeptical problems, those who lived during the Renaissance and early modern periods (approximately the 16th and 17th centuries) were positively obsessed by them. The rediscovery of much ancient Greek literature and philosophy by Italian humanists starting in the 12th century brought with it a keen appreciation of ancient Skepticism, including as it pertained to ethics. In the 17th and early 18th centuries, a group of English philosophers known as the Cambridge Platonists developed the theory that moral truths are known through a kind of rational intuition, similar to the intuition through which mathematical truths are known (a view briefly revived in the early 20th century). British philosophers of the 18th century took an empiricist tack by positing a special "moral sense," based on natural feelings such as benevolence, that is pleased by what is morally right and offended by what is morally wrong. Moral sense theory also suggested a solution to the problem of why one should be moral, assuming that it is in one's self-interest to behave in ways that please one's own moral sense.

Political philosophers such as Thomas Hobbes (1588–1679) and John Locke (1632–1704) had earlier proposed that moral behaviour is in one's self-interest because morality consists of a "social contract" in which each member of society agrees to surrender some measure of his right to pursue his self-interest in return for a similar concession from everyone else. In other words, morality is a system of reciprocal obligations born of the necessity to preserve peace and order. Social-contract theory was relatively neglected during the 19th century but was subsequently revived, becoming a major theme in metaethics starting in the second half of the 20th century.

All three of these guiding metaethical questions—regarding objectivity, knowledge, and self-interest—were addressed in the ethical philosophy of Immanuel Kant (1724–1804), who is perhaps the most important moral philosopher after Aristotle. In normative ethics Kant was also the leading expositor of deontology, or rule-based ethics, the main historical rival of consequentialism.

According to Kant, right actions are those that one can consistently will to become a universal law (i.e., a law that is followed by everyone). A law is willed "consistently" if, in willing it, one does not contradict or undermine the object of one's will. Thus it is wrong to make false promises because the universal practice of making false promises would destroy the institution of promise making, thereby ensuring that one's own false promises would not succeed. For Kant, moral laws are objective in the sense that they are valid for all rational beings, and they are knowable because it is immediately evident whether the standard of universalizability applies. It is less clear how moral laws are consistent with the agent's self-interest, but one possibility is that by willing what is universalizable, one wills on the basis of reason alone (rather than on the basis of desire), and it is only when one wills on the basis of reason alone that one is truly free. Kant's ethical philosophy was influential in the early and later parts of the 19th century, and it has been a major current in normative ethics and metaethics since the mid-20th century.

These metaethical questions continued to guide much ethical theorizing in the 20th century. They became the topic of much discussion even outside philosophy with the advent in the 1970s of postmodernism, an approach to literature and philosophy that challenged allegedly outmoded aspirations, inherited from the Enlightenment, regarding the discovery of truth, the understanding of history, and the possibility of human moral and material progress. Although the most extreme assertions of postmodernism are no longer taken seriously, its basic stance of relativism and skepticism remains important in continental European philosophy and in some Anglo-American philosophical schools, notably feminism.

Starting in the 1960s and '70s, ethical philosophy in the English-speaking world began to pay much more attention to real-life moral problems, including medical dilemmas as well as issues related to war and peace, the environment, and the treatment of animals. Applied ethics is now by far the most popular and practically influential field of philosophy.

Morality is certainly a pervasive aspect of human life. Human beings constantly perceive and assess the world, each other, and themselves in moral terms. Indeed, people usually regard their moral values as an important part of their identity. By becoming acquainted with the ideas in this book, therefore, you can enrich your experience of life and come to understand yourself that much better.

CHAPTER 1

THE NATURE AND ORIGINS OF ETHICS

How should we live? What should we value most in life? Should we aim at happiness, knowledge, virtue, or the creation of beautiful objects? If we choose happiness, will it be our own or the happiness of all? And what of the more particular questions that face us: is it right to be dishonest in a good cause? Can we justify living in opulence while elsewhere in the world people starve? Is going to war justified in cases where it is likely that innocent people will be killed? Is it wrong to clone a human being or to destroy human embryos in medical research? What are our obligations, if any, to the generations of humans who will come after us and to the nonhuman animals with whom we share the planet?

Ethics, also called moral philosophy, considers questions such as these at all levels. It can be defined as the study of what is morally good, right, or just and of what is morally bad, wrong, or unjust. Its major concerns include the nature of ultimate moral value and the standards by which actions, individuals, or states of affairs can be morally evaluated. The term *ethics* is also used to refer to any system or theory of moral values or principles, as in *the ethics of Aristotle* or *Jewish ethics*.

Although ethics has always been viewed as a branch of philosophy, its all-embracing practical nature links it with many other areas of study, including anthropology, biology, economics, history, politics, sociology, and theology. Yet, ethics remains distinct from such disciplines because it is not a matter of factual knowledge in the way that the sciences and other branches of inquiry are. Rather, it has to do with determining the nature of normative theories, which are concerned with standards or norms of conduct, and applying these principles to practical moral problems.

THE INTRODUCTION OF MORAL CODES

When did ethics begin and how did it originate? If one has in mind ethics proper (i.e., the systematic study of what is morally right and wrong), it is clear that ethics could have come into existence only when human beings started to reflect on the best way to live. This reflective stage emerged long after human societies had developed some kind of morality, usually in the form of customary standards of right and wrong conduct. The process of reflection tended to arise from such customs, even if in the end it may have found them wanting. Accordingly, ethics began with the introduction of the first moral codes.

MYTHICAL ACCOUNTS

Virtually every human society has some form of myth to explain the origin of morality. In the Louvre Museum in Paris there is a black Babylonian column with a relief showing the sun god Shamash presenting the code of laws to Hammurabi (died *c.* 1750 BCE), known as the Code of Hammurabi. Another example might be the account in the Hebrew Bible (Old Testament) of God's giving the Ten Commandments to Moses (flourished 14th–13th century BCE) on Mount Sinai. The dialogue *Protagoras* by the Greek philosopher Plato (428/27–348/47 BCE), gives an avowedly mythical account of how the god Zeus took pity on the hapless humans, who were physically no match for the other beasts. To make up for their deficiencies, Zeus gave humans a moral sense and the capacity for law and justice, so that they could live in larger communities and cooperate with one another.

That morality should be invested with all the mystery and power of divine origin is not surprising. Nothing else could provide such strong reasons for accepting the moral law. By attributing a divine origin to morality, the priesthood became its interpreter and guardian and thereby secured for itself a power that it would not readily relinquish. This link between morality and religion has been so firmly forged that it is still sometimes asserted that there can be no morality without religion. According to this view, ethics is not an independent field of study but rather a branch of theology.

There is some difficulty, already known to Plato, with the view that morality was created by a divine power.

Detail of the stela inscribed with the Code of Hammurabi showing the king before the god Shamash. Bas-relief from Susa, 18th century BCE, in the Louvre, Paris. Courtesy of the trustees of the British Museum; photograph, J.R. Freeman & Co. Ltd.

In his dialogue *Euthyphro*, Plato considered the suggestion that it is divine approval that makes an action good. Plato pointed out that, if this were the case, one could not say that the gods approve of such actions because they are good. Why then do they approve of them? Is their approval entirely arbitrary? Plato considered this impossible and so held that there must be some standards of right or wrong that are independent of the likes and dislikes of the gods. Modern philosophers have generally accepted Plato's argument, because the alternative implies that if, for example, the gods had happened to

Code of Hammurabi

The Code of Hammurabi is the most complete and perfect extant collection of Babylonian laws. Developed during the reign of Hammurabi (1792–50 BCE) of the 1st dynasty of Babylon, it consists of his legal decisions that were collected toward the end of his reign and inscribed on a diorite stela set up in Babylon's temple of Marduk, the national god of Babylonia. These 282 case laws include economic provisions (prices, tariffs, trade, and commerce), family law (marriage and divorce), as well as criminal law (assault and theft) and civil law (slavery and debt). Penalties varied according to the status of the offenders and the circumstances of the offenses.

The background of the code is a body of Sumerian law under which civilized communities had lived for many centuries. The existing text is in the Akkadian (Semitic) language. Although no Sumerian version is known to survive, the code was intended to be applied to a wider realm than any single country and to integrate Semitic and Sumerian traditions and peoples. Moreover, despite a few primitive survivals relating to family solidarity, district responsibility, trial by ordeal, and the *lex talionis* (Latin: "law of retaliation," i.e., an eye for an eye, a tooth for a tooth), the code was advanced far beyond tribal custom and recognized no blood feud, private retribution, or marriage by capture.

The principal (and only considerable) source of the Code of Hammurabi is the stela discovered at Susa in 1901 by the French Orientalist Jean-Vincent Scheil and now preserved in the Louvre.

approve of torturing children and disapprove of helping one's neighbours, torture would have been good and
neighbourliness bad.

PROBLEMS OF DIVINE ORIGIN

A modern theist might say that, because God is good, God
could not possibly approve of torturing children nor disapprove of helping neighbours. In saying this, however, the
theist would have tacitly admitted that there is a standard
of goodness that is independent of God. Without an independent standard, it would be pointless to say that God
is good. This could mean only that God is approved of by
God. It seems therefore that, even for those who believe
in the existence of God, it is impossible to give a satisfac-
tory account of the origin of morality in terms of divine
creation. A different account is needed.

There are other possible connections between religion and morality. It has been said that, even if standards
of good and evil exist independently of God or the gods,
divine revelation is the only reliable means of finding out
what these standards are. An obvious problem with this
view is that those who receive divine revelations, or who
consider themselves qualified to interpret them, do not
always agree on what is good and what is evil. Without an
accepted criterion for the authenticity of a revelation or
an interpretation, people are no better off, so far as reaching moral agreement is concerned, than they would be if
they were to decide on good and evil themselves, with no
assistance from religion.

Traditionally, a more important link between religion
and ethics was that religious teachings were thought to
provide a reason for doing what is right. In its crudest
form, the reason was that those who obey the moral law
will be rewarded by an eternity of bliss while everyone else

roasts in hell. In more sophisticated versions, the motivation provided by religion was more inspirational and less blatantly self-interested. Whether in its crude or its sophisticated version, or something in between, religion does provide an answer to one of the great questions of ethics: "Why should I be moral?" As will be seen in the course of this book, however, the answer provided by religion is not the only one available.

PREHUMAN ETHICS

Because, for obvious reasons, there is no historical record of a human society in the period before it had any standards of right and wrong, history cannot reveal the origins of morality. Nor is anthropology of any help, because all the human societies that have been studied so far had their own forms of morality (except perhaps in the most extreme circumstances). Fortunately, another mode of inquiry is available. Because living in social groups is a characteristic that humans share with many other animal species—including their closest relatives, the apes—presumably the common ancestor of humans and apes also lived in social groups. Here, then, in the social behaviour of nonhuman animals and in the theory of evolution that explains such behaviour may be found the origins of human morality.

NONHUMAN BEHAVIOUR

Social life, even for nonhuman animals, requires constraints on behaviour. No group can stay together if its members make frequent, unrestrained attacks on each other. With some exceptions, social animals generally either refrain altogether from attacking other members of the social group or, if an attack does take place, do not make the ensuing struggle a fight to the death—it is over when the weaker animal shows submissive behaviour. It is not difficult to see analogies here with human moral codes. The parallels, however, go much further than this. Like humans, social animals may behave in ways that benefit other members of the group at some cost or risk to themselves. Male baboons threaten predators and cover the rear as the troop retreats. Wolves and wild dogs take meat back to members of the pack not present at the kill. Gibbons and chimpanzees with food will, in response to a gesture, share their food with other members of the group. Dolphins support other sick or injured dolphins, swimming under them for hours at a time and pushing them to the surface so they can breathe.

Social animals often act to benefit other members of their group. For example, wolves take meat to pack members not present at a kill. © www.istockphoto .com/Len Tillim

It may be thought that the existence of such apparently altruistic behaviour is odd, for evolutionary theory states that those who do not struggle to survive and reproduce will be eliminated through natural selection. Research in evolutionary theory applied to social behaviour, however, has shown that evolution need not be so ruthless. Some altruistic behaviour is explained by kin selection. The most obvious examples are those in which parents make sacrifices for their offspring. If wolves help their cubs to survive, it is more likely that genetic characteristics, including the characteristic of helping their own cubs, will spread through further generations of wolves.

KINSHIP AND RECIPROCITY

Less obviously, the principle also holds for assistance to other close relatives, even if they are not descendants. A child shares 50 percent of the genes of each of its parents, but full siblings too, on the average, have 50 percent of their genes in common. Thus, a tendency to sacrifice one's life for two or more of one's siblings could spread from one generation to the next. Between cousins, where only 12.5 percent of the genes are shared, the benefit-to-sacrifice ratio would have to be correspondingly increased.

When apparent altruism is not between kin, it may be based on reciprocity. A monkey will present its back to another monkey, which will pick out parasites, and after a time the roles will be reversed. Reciprocity may also be a factor in food sharing among unrelated animals. Such reciprocity will pay off, in evolutionary terms, as long as the costs of helping are less than the benefits of being helped and as long as animals will not gain in the long run by "cheating"—that is to say, by receiving favours without returning them. It would seem that the best way to ensure that those that cheat do not prosper is for animals to be able to recognize cheats and refuse them the benefits of cooperation the next time around. This is possible only among intelligent animals living in small, stable groups over a long period of time. Evidence supports this conclusion: reciprocal behaviour has been observed in birds and mammals, the clearest cases occurring among wolves, wild dogs, dolphins, monkeys, and apes.

In short, kin altruism and reciprocity do exist, at least in some nonhuman animals living in groups. Could these forms of behaviour be the basis of human ethics? There are good reasons for believing that they could. Kinship is a source of obligation in every human society. A mother's duty to look after her children is recognized in every known society, and the duty of a father to support and protect his family is almost as widely maintained. Duties to close relatives take priority over duties to more distant relatives, but in most societies even distant relatives are still treated better than strangers.

If kinship is the most basic and universal tie between human beings, the bond of reciprocity is not far behind. It would be difficult to find a society that did not recognize, at least under some circumstances, an obligation to return favours. In many cultures this is taken to extraordinary lengths, and there are elaborate rituals of gift giving. Often the repayment must be superior to the original gift, and this escalation can reach extremes that eventually threaten the economic security of the donor. The huge potlatch, feasts of certain Native American tribes are a well-known example of this type of situation. Many Melanesian societies also place great importance on giving and receiving substantial amounts of valuable items.

Many features of human morality could have grown out of simple reciprocal practices, such as the mutual removal of parasites from awkward places. Suppose a person wanted to have the lice in his hair picked out and was willing in return to remove lice from someone else's hair. The person must choose his partner carefully. If he helps everyone indiscriminately, he will find himself delousing others without getting his own lice removed. To avoid this, he must learn to distinguish between those who return favours and those who do not. In making this distinction, he would be separating reciprocators from nonreciprocators and, in the process, developing crude notions of fairness and of cheating. He will naturally strengthen his ties to those who reciprocate, and bonds of friendship and loyalty, with a consequent sense of obligation to assist, will result.

This is not all. The reciprocators are likely to react in a hostile and angry way to those who do not reciprocate.

Investors believed they were entering into a reciprocal relationship with Bernard Madoff (centre), who instead swindled them out of billions of dollars. Chris Hondros/Getty Images

Perhaps they will regard reciprocity as good and "right" and cheating as bad and "wrong." From here it is a small step to concluding that the worst of the nonreciprocators should be driven out of society or else punished in some way so that they will not take advantage of others again. Thus, a system of punishment and a notion of just desert constitute the other side of reciprocal altruism.

Although kinship and reciprocity loom large in human morality, they do not cover the entire field. Typically, there are obligations to other members of the village, tribe, or nation, even when they are strangers. There may also be a loyalty to the group as a whole that is distinct from loyalty to individual members of the group. It may be at this point that human culture intervenes. Each society has a clear interest in promoting devotion to the group and can be expected to develop cultural influences that exalt those who make sacrifices for the sake of the group and revile those who put their own interests too far ahead. More tangible rewards and punishments may supplement the persuasive effect of social opinion. This is the start of a process of cultural development of moral codes.

Research in psychology and the neurosciences has thrown light on the role of specific parts of the brain in moral judgment and behaviour, suggesting that emotions are strongly involved in moral judgments, particularly those that are formed rapidly and intuitively. These emotions could be the result of social and cultural influences, or they could have a biological basis in the evolutionary history of the human species. Such a basis would continue to exert some influence even if social and cultural forces pulled in different directions. Some research, however, also indicates that people sometimes use reasoning processes to reach moral judgments that contradict their usual intuitive responses.

ANTHROPOLOGY AND ETHICS

Many people believe that there are no moral universals (i.e., that there is so much variation from one culture to another that no single moral principle or judgment is generally accepted). It has already been shown that this is not the case. Of course, there are immense differences in the way in which the broad principles so far discussed are applied. The duty of children to their parents meant one thing in traditional Chinese society and means something quite different in contemporary Western societies. Yet, concern for kin and reciprocity are considered good in virtually all human societies. Also, all societies have, for obvious reasons, some constraints on killing and wounding other members of the group.

Beyond this common ground, the variations in moral attitudes soon become more striking than the similarities. People have been fascinated with such variations since ancient times. The Greek historian Herodotus (died 430–420 BCE) relates that the Persian king Darius I (550–486 BCE) once summoned some Greeks before him and asked them how much he would have to pay them to eat their fathers' dead bodies. They refused to do it at any price. Then he summoned some Indians who by custom ate the bodies of their parents and asked them what would make them willing to burn their fathers' bodies. The Indians cried out that he should not mention so horrid an act. Herodotus drew the obvious moral: each nation thinks its own customs best.

Variations in morals were not systematically studied until the 19th century, when Western knowledge of the more remote parts of the globe began to increase. In *The Origin and Development of the Moral Ideas* (1906–08), the Finnish anthropologist Edward Westermarck (1862–1939) compared differences between societies in matters such as the wrongness of killing (including killing in warfare, euthanasia, suicide, infanticide, abortion, human sacrifice, and duelling); the duty to support children, the aged, or the poor; forms of permissible sexual relationship; the status of women; the right to property and what constitutes theft; the holding of slaves; the duty to tell the truth; dietary restrictions; concern for nonhuman animals; duties to the dead; and duties to the gods. Westermarck had no difficulty in demonstrating tremendous diversity in what different societies considered good conduct in all these areas. More recent, though less comprehensive, studies have confirmed that human societies can and do flourish while holding radically different views about all such matters—though of course various

Aaron Burr killed Alexander Hamilton in a duel at a time when such often-fatal standoffs were considered an acceptable means of settling disagreements. Kean Collection/Hulton Archive/Getty Images

groups within a society may do less well under some sets of beliefs than others.

As noted earlier, ethics itself is not primarily concerned with the description of the moral systems of different societies. That task, which remains on the level of description, is one for anthropology or sociology. In contrast, ethics deals with the justification of moral principles (or with the impossibility of such a justification). Nevertheless, ethics must take note of the variations in moral systems, because it has often been claimed that this variety shows that morality is simply a matter of what is customary and that it thus is always relative to particular societies. According to this view, no moral principle can be valid except in the societies in which it is held. Words such as *good* and *bad* just mean, it is claimed, "approved in my society" or "disapproved in my society," and so to search for an objective, or rationally justifiable, ethics is to search for what is in fact an illusion.

One way of replying to this position would be to stress the fact that there are some features common to virtually all human moralities. It might be thought that these common features must be the universally valid and objective core of morality. This argument would, however, involve a fallacy. If the explanation for the common features is simply that they are advantageous in terms of evolutionary theory, that does not make them right. Evolution is a blind force incapable of conferring a moral imprimatur on human behaviour. It may be a fact that concern for kin is in accord with evolutionary theory, but to say that concern for kin is therefore right would be to attempt to deduce values from facts. In any case, the fact that something is universally approved does not make it right. If all human societies enslaved any tribe they could conquer, and some freethinking moralists nevertheless insisted that slavery is wrong, they could not be said to be talking nonsense merely because they had few supporters. Similarly, then, universal support for principles of kinship and reciprocity cannot prove that these principles are in some way objectively justified.

This example illustrates the way in which ethics differs from the descriptive sciences. From the standpoint of ethics, whether human moral codes closely parallel one another or are extraordinarily diverse, the question of how an individual should act remains open. People who are uncertain about what they should do will not be helped by being told what their society thinks they should do in the circumstances in which they find themselves. Even if they are told that virtually all other human societies agree and that this agreement stems from evolved human nature, they may still reasonably choose to act otherwise. If they are told that there is great variation between human societies regarding what people should do in such circumstances, they may wonder whether there can be any objective answer, but their dilemma still would not be resolved. In fact, this diversity does not rule out the possibility of an objective answer: conceivably, most societies simply got it wrong. This too is something that will be taken up later in this book, for the possibility of an objective morality is one of the constant themes of ethics.

CHAPTER 2

ETHICS IN THE ANCIENT WORLD

The first ethical precepts must have been passed down by word of mouth from parents and elders, but as societies learned to use the written word, they began to set down their ethical beliefs. These records constitute the earliest known evidence of what could be called a system of ethics.

THE MIDDLE EAST

The earliest surviving writings that might be taken as ethics textbooks are a series of lists of precepts to be learned by boys of the ruling class of Egypt, prepared some 3,000 years before the Common Era. In most cases, they consist of shrewd advice on how to live happily, avoid unnecessary troubles, and advance one's career by cultivating the favour of superiors. There are, however, several passages that recommend more broadly based ideals of conduct, such as the following: rulers should treat their people justly and judge impartially between their subjects; they should aim to make their people prosperous; those who have bread should share it with the hungry; humble and lowly people must be treated with kindness; one should not laugh at the blind or at dwarfs.

Why, then, should one follow these precepts? Did the ancient Egyptians believe that one should do what

Modern society follows many of the axioms taught by the Egyptians thousands of years before the Common Era, such as those with food should share it with the hungry. Sean Gallup/Getty Images

is good for its own sake? The precepts frequently state that it will profit a man to act justly, as in the maxim "Honesty is the best policy." They also emphasize the importance of having a good name. These precepts were intended for the instruction of the ruling classes, however, and it is unclear why helping the destitute should have contributed to an individual's good reputation among this class. To some degree, therefore, the authors of the precepts must have thought that to make people prosperous and happy and to be kind to those who have least is not merely personally advantageous but good in itself.

The precepts are not works of ethics in the philosophical sense. No attempt is made to find any underlying principles of conduct that might provide a more systematic understanding of ethics. Justice, for example, is given a prominent place, but there is no elaboration of the notion of justice or any discussion of how disagreements about what is just and unjust might be resolved. Furthermore, there is no probing of ethical dilemmas that may occur if the precepts should conflict with one another. The precepts are full of sound observations and practical wisdom, but they do not encourage theoretical speculation.

The same practical bent can be found in other early codes or lists of ethical injunctions. The Code of Hammurabi is often said to have been based on the principle of "an eye for an eye, a tooth for a tooth"—as if this were some fundamental principle of justice, elaborated and applied to all cases. In fact, the code reflects no such consistent principle. It frequently prescribes the death penalty for offenses that do not themselves cause death (e.g., robbery and accepting bribes). Moreover, even the eye-for-an-eye rule applies only if the eye of the original victim is that of a member of the patrician class. If it is the eye of a commoner, the punishment is a fine of a quantity of silver. Apparently, such differences in punishment were not thought to require justification. At any rate, there are no surviving attempts to defend the principles of justice on which the code was based.

The Hebrew people were at different times captives of both the Egyptians and the Babylonians. It is therefore not surprising that the law of ancient Israel, which was put into its definitive form during the Babylonian Exile (6th century BCE), shows the influence both of the ancient Egyptian precepts and of the Code of Hammurabi. The book of Exodus refers, for example, to the principle of "life for life, eye for eye, tooth for tooth." Hebraic law does not differentiate, as the Babylonian law does, between patricians and commoners, but it does stipulate that in several respects foreigners may be treated in ways that it is not permissible to treat fellow Hebrews. For instance, Hebrew slaves, but not others, had to be freed without ransom in the seventh year. Yet, in other respects Hebraic law and morality developed the humane concern shown in the Egyptian precepts for the poor and unfortunate: hired servants must be paid promptly, because they rely on their wages to satisfy their pressing needs; slaves must be allowed to rest on the seventh day; widows, orphans, and the blind and deaf must not be wronged; and the poor man should not be refused a loan. There was even a tithe providing for an incipient welfare state. The spirit of this humane concern was summed up by the injunction to "love thy neighbour as thyself," a sweepingly generous form of the rule of reciprocity.

The famed Ten Commandments are thought to be a legacy of Semitic tribal law from a time when important commands were taught one for each finger, so they could be remembered more easily (sets of five or 10 laws are common among preliterate civilizations). The content of the Hebrew commandments differed from other laws of the region mainly in its emphasis on duties to God. This emphasis persisted in the more detailed laws laid down elsewhere. As much as half of such legislation was concerned with crimes against God and ceremonial and ritualistic matters, but there may be other explanations for some of these ostensibly religious requirements concerning the avoidance of certain foods and the need for ceremonial cleansings.

In addition to lengthy statements of the law, the surviving literature of ancient Israel includes both proverbs and the books of the prophets. The proverbs, like the precepts of the Egyptians, are brief statements that do not demonstrate much concern for systematic presentation or overall coherence. They go farther than the Egyptian precepts, however, in urging conduct that is just and upright and pleasing to God. Although correspondingly fewer references exist regarding what is needed for a successful career, it is frequently stated that God rewards the just. In this connection, the book of Job is notable as an exploration of the problem raised for those who accept this motive for obeying the moral law: why do the best of people frequently suffer the worst misfortunes? The book offers no solution beyond faith in God, but the sharpened awareness of the problem it offers may have influenced some to adopt the belief in reward and punishment in another realm as the only possible solution.

The literature of the prophets contains a good deal of social and moral criticism, but most of it consists of denunciation rather than discussion about what goodness really is or why there should be so much wrongdoing. The book of Isaiah is especially notable for its early portrayal of a utopia in which "the desert shall blossom as the rose... the wolf also shall dwell with the lamb....They shall not hurt or destroy in all my holy mountain."

INDIA

Unlike the ethical teachings of ancient Egypt and Babylonia, Indian ethics was philosophical from the start. In the oldest of the Indian writings, the Vedas, ethics is an integral aspect of philosophical and religious speculation about the nature of reality. These writings, dating from about 1500 BCE, have been described as the oldest philosophical literature in the world, and what they say about how people ought to live may therefore be the first philosophical ethics.

The Vedas are, in a sense, hymns, but the gods to which they refer are not persons but manifestations of ultimate truth and reality. In the Vedic philosophy, the basic principle of the universe, the ultimate reality on which the cosmos exists, is the principle of *Ritam*, which is the word from which the Western notion of right is derived. There is thus a belief in a right moral order somehow built into the universe itself. Hence, truth and right are linked; to penetrate through illusion and understand the ultimate truth of human existence is to understand what is right. To be an enlightened person is to know what is real and to live rightly, for these are not two separate things but one and the same.

The ethics that is thus traced to the very essence of the universe is not without detailed practical applications. These applications were based on four ideals, or proper goals, of life: prosperity, the satisfaction of desires, moral duty, and spiritual perfection (i.e., liberation from a finite existence). From these ends follow certain virtues: honesty, rectitude, charity, nonviolence, modesty, and purity of heart. Conversely, to be condemned are falsehood, egoism, cruelty, adultery, theft, and injury to living things. Because the eternal moral law is part of the universe, to do what is praiseworthy is to act in harmony with the universe, and accordingly such action will receive its proper reward. Once the true nature of the self is understood, however, it becomes apparent that those who do what is wrong are acting self-destructively.

These basic principles underwent considerable modification over the ensuing centuries, especially in the Upanishads, a body of philosophical literature dating from 800 BCE. The Indian caste system, with its intricate laws about what members of each caste may or may not do, is accepted by the Upanishads as part of the proper order of the universe. Ethics itself, however, is not regarded as a matter of conformity to laws. Instead, the desire to be ethical is an inner desire. It is part of the quest for spiritual perfection, which in turn is elevated to the highest of the four goals of life.

During the following centuries, the moral philosophy of this early period gradually became a rigid and dogmatic system that provoked several reactions. One, which is uncharacteristic of Indian thought in general, was the Carvaka, or materialist school, which mocked religious ceremonies, saying that they were invented by the Brahmans (the priestly caste) to ensure their livelihood. When the Brahmans defended animal sacrifices by claiming that the sacrificed beast goes straight to heaven, the members of the Carvaka asked why the Brahmans did not kill their aged parents to hasten their arrival there. Against the postulation of an eventual spiritual liberation, Carvaka ethics urged each individual to seek his or her pleasure in the here and now.

Jainism, another reaction to the traditional Vedic outlook, reached exactly the opposite conclusions. The Jain philosophy is based on spiritual liberation as the highest of all goals and ahimsa (noninjury or nonviolence) as the means of attaining it. In true philosophical manner, the Jains found in the principle of noninjury a guide to all morality. First, apart from the obvious application to prohibiting violent acts directed at other humans, noninjury is extended to all living things. The Jains are vegetarian. They are often ridiculed by Westerners for the care they take to avoid injuring insects or other living things while walking or drinking water that may contain minute organisms. Less well known is the fact that Jains began to care for sick and injured animals thousands of years before animal shelters were thought of in Europe. The Jains do not draw the distinction usually made in Western ethics between their responsibility for what they do and their responsibility for what they omit doing. They would also view omitting to care for an injured animal as a form of violence.

Other moral duties are also derived from the notion of noninjury. To tell someone a lie, for example, is regarded

Often ridiculed for their efforts to avoid harming organisms of any size, Jains tended to sick and injured animals thousands of years before European animal shelters came to be. Dibyangshu Sarkar/AFP/Getty Images

as inflicting a mental injury on that person. Stealing, of course, is another form of injury, but because of the absence of a distinction between acts and omissions, even the possession of wealth is seen as depriving the poor and hungry of the means to satisfy their wants. Thus, noninjury leads to a principle of nonpossession of property. Jain priests were expected to be strict ascetics and to avoid sexual intercourse. Ordinary Jains, however, followed a slightly less severe code, which was intended to give effect to the major forms of noninjury while still being compatible with a normal life.

The other great ethical system to develop as a reaction to the ossified form of the old Vedic philosophy was Buddhism. The person who became known as the Buddha (flourished *c.* 6th–4th century BCE), which means the "enlightened one," was born the son of a king. Until he was 29 years old, he lived the sheltered life of a typical prince, with every luxury he could desire. At that time, legend has it, he was jolted out of his idleness by the "Four Signs": he saw in succession an old man, a sick person, a corpse being carried to cremation, and a monk in meditation beneath a tree. He began to think about old age, disease, and death, and decided to follow the way of the monk. For six years he led an ascetic life of renunciation. Finally, while meditating under a tree, he concluded that the solution was not withdrawal from the world, but rather a practical life of compassion for all.

Buddhism is conventionally regarded as a religion, and indeed over the centuries it adopted religious trappings in many places. This is an irony of history, however, because the Buddha himself was a strong critic of religion. He rejected the authority of the Vedas and refused to set up an alternative creed, regarded religious ceremonies as a waste of time, and considered theological beliefs as mere superstition. He refused to discuss abstract metaphysical problems such as the immortality of the soul. The Buddha told his followers to think for themselves and take responsibility for their own future. In place of religious beliefs and religious ceremonies, the Buddha advocated a life devoted to universal compassion and brotherhood. Through such a life one might reach the ultimate goal, Nirvana, a state in which all living things are free from pain and sorrow. There are similarities between this morality of universal compassion and the ethics of the Jains.

In keeping with his own previous experience, the Buddha proposed a "middle path" between self-indulgence and self-renunciation. In fact, it is not so much a path between these two extremes as one that draws together the benefits of both. Through living a life of compassion and love for all, a person achieves the liberation from selfish cravings sought by the ascetic and a serenity and satisfaction that are more fulfilling than anything obtained by indulgence in pleasure.

It is sometimes thought that because the Buddhist goal is Nirvana, a state that can be reached by meditation, Buddhism teaches a withdrawal from the real world. Nirvana, however, is not to be sought for oneself alone; it is regarded as a unity of the individual self with the universal self in which all things take part. In the Mahayana school of Buddhism, the aspirant to enlightenment even takes a vow not to accept final release until everything that exists in the universe has attained Nirvana.

The Buddha lived and taught in India, so Buddhism is properly classified as an Indian moral philosophy. Yet, Buddhism did not take hold in the land of its origin. Instead, it spread in different forms south into Sri Lanka and Southeast Asia and north through Tibet to China, Korea, and Japan. In the process, Buddhism suffered the same fate as the Vedic philosophy against which it had rebelled: it became a religion, often rigid, with its own sects, ceremonies, and superstitions.

Ahimsa

Ahimsa, originally a Sanskrit term meaning noninjury or nonviolence, is the fundamental ethical virtue of the Jains of India and is also highly respected among Hindus and Buddhists. In the early 20th century Mahatma Gandhi, the leader of the Indian nationalist movement against British rule, extended ahimsa into the political sphere as satyagraha, the principle of nonviolent resistance to evil or injustice.

In Jainism, ahimsa is the standard by which all actions are judged. For a householder observing the "small vows" (*anuvrata*), the practice of ahimsa requires that he not kill any animal life, but for an ascetic observing the "great vows" (*mahāvrata*), ahimsa entails the greatest care to prevent him from knowingly or unknowingly being the cause of injury to any living substance. Living matter (*jīva*) includes not only human beings and animals but insects, plants, and atoms as well, and the same law governs the entire cosmos. The interruption of another *jīva*'s spiritual progress increases one's own karma and delays one's liberation from the cycle of rebirths. Many common Jainist practices, such as not eating or drinking after dark or the wearing of cloth mouth covers (*mukhavastrikā*) by monks, are based on the principle of ahimsa.

Although the Hindus and Buddhists never required so strict an observance of ahimsa as the Jains, vegetarianism and tolerance toward all forms of life became widespread in India. The inscriptions of the Buddhist emperor Ashoka (died *c.* 238 BCE) stressed the sanctity of animal life. Ahimsa is one of the first disciplines learned by the student of yoga and is required to be mastered in the preparatory stage (*yama*), the first of the eight stages that lead to perfect concentration.

CHINA

The two greatest moral philosophers of ancient China, Laozi (flourished *c.* 6th century BCE) and Confucius (551–479 BCE), thought in very different ways. Laozi is best known for his ideas about the Dao (literally, the "Way," or Supreme Principle). The Dao is based on the traditional Chinese virtues of simplicity and sincerity. To follow the

Dao is a matter not of observing any set of duties or prohibitions but rather of living in a simple and honest manner, being true to oneself, and avoiding the distractions of ordinary living. Laozi's classic book on the Dao, *Daodejing*, consists only of aphorisms and isolated paragraphs, making it difficult to draw an intelligible system of ethics from it. Perhaps this is because Laozi was a type of moral skeptic: he rejected both righteousness and benevolence, apparently because he saw them as imposed on individuals from without rather than coming from their own inner natures. Like the Buddha, Laozi found the things prized by the world—rank, luxury, and glamour—to be empty and worthless when compared with the ultimate value of a peaceful inner life. He also emphasized gentleness, calm, and nonviolence. Nearly 600 years before Jesus, he said: "It is the way of the Dao...to recompense injury with kindness." By returning good for good and also good for evil, Laozi believed that all would become good; to return evil for evil would lead to chaos.

The lives of Laozi and Confucius overlapped, and there is even an account of a meeting between them, which is said to have left the younger Confucius baffled. Confucius was the more down-to-earth thinker, absorbed in the practical task of social reform. The province in which he served as minister of justice became renowned for the honesty of its people, the respect shown to the aged, and the care taken of the poor. Probably because of their practical nature, the teachings of Confucius had a far greater influence on China than did those of the more withdrawn Laozi.

Confucius did not organize his recommendations into any coherent system. His teachings are offered in the form of sayings, aphorisms, and anecdotes, usually in reply to questions by disciples. They aim at guiding the student toward becoming a better person, a concept translated as "gentleman" or "the superior man." In opposition to the prevailing feudal ideal of the aristocratic lord, Confucius presented the superior man as one who is humane and thoughtful, motivated by the desire to do what is good rather than by personal profit. Beyond this, however, the concept is not discussed in any detail; it is only shown by diverse examples, some of them trite: "A superior man's life leads upwards....The superior man is broad and fair; the inferior man takes sides and is petty....A superior man shapes the good in man; he does not shape the bad in him."

One of the recorded sayings of Confucius is an answer to a request from a disciple for a single word that could serve as a guide to conduct for one's entire life. He replied: "Is not reciprocity such a word? What you do not want done to yourself, do not do to others." This rule is repeated several times in the Confucian literature and might be considered the supreme principle of Confucian ethics. Other duties are not, however, presented as derivative from this supreme principle, nor is the principle used to determine what should be done when two or more specific duties— e.g., the duty to parents and the duty to friends, both of which are prominent in Confucian ethics—conflict with each other.

Confucius did not explain why the superior man chooses righteousness rather than personal profit. This question was taken up more than 100 years after his death by his follower Mencius (c. 372–c. 289 BCE), who asserted that humans are naturally inclined to do what is humane and right. Evil is not part of human nature but is the result of poor upbringing or lack of education. But Confucius also had another distinguished follower, Xunzi (c. 300–c. 230 BCE), who said that humans naturally seek profit for themselves and envy others. The rules of morality are designed to avoid the strife that would otherwise follow from acting according to this nature. The Confucian school was united in its ideal of the superior man but divided over whether such an ideal was to be obtained by controlling people's natural desires or allowing them to be fulfilled.

ANCIENT GREECE

Ancient Greece was the birthplace of Western philosophical ethics. The ideas of Socrates (*c.* 470–399 BCE), Plato, and Aristotle (384–322 BCE) will be discussed in the next section. The sudden flowering of philosophy during that period was rooted in the ethical thought of earlier centuries. In the poetic literature of the 7th and 6th centuries BCE, there were, as in other cultures, moral precepts but no real attempts to formulate a coherent overall ethical position. The Greeks were later to refer to the most prominent of these poets and early philosophers as the seven sages, and they are frequently quoted with respect by Plato and Aristotle. Knowledge of the thought of this period is limited, for often only fragments of original writings, along with later accounts of dubious accuracy, remain.

Pythagoras (*c.* 580–*c.* 500 BCE), whose name is familiar because of the geometric theorem that bears his name, is one such early Greek thinker about whom little is known. He appears to have written nothing at all, but he was the founder of a school of thought that touched on all aspects of life and that may have been a kind of philosophical and religious order. In ancient times the school was best known for its advocacy of vegetarianism, which, like that of the Jains, was associated with the belief that after the death of the body, the human soul may take up residence in the body of an animal. Pythagoreans continued to espouse this view for many centuries, and classical passages in the works of writers such as Ovid (43 BCE–17 CE) and Porphyry (234–305 CE) opposing bloodshed and animal slaughter can be traced to Pythagoras.

Ironically, an important stimulus for the development of moral philosophy came from a group of teachers to whom the later Greek philosophers—Socrates, Plato, and Aristotle—were consistently hostile: the Sophists. This term was used in the 5th century BCE to refer to a class of professional teachers of rhetoric and argument. The Sophists promised their pupils success in political debate and increased influence in the affairs of the city. They were accused of being mercenaries who taught their students how to win arguments, whether by fair means or foul. Aristotle said that Protagoras (c. 485–c. 410 BCE), perhaps the most famous of the Sophists, claimed to teach how "to make the weaker argument the stronger."

The Sophists, however, were more than mere teachers of rhetorical tricks. They regarded themselves as imparters of the cultural and intellectual qualities necessary for success, and their involvement with argument about practical affairs naturally led them to develop views about ethics. The recurrent theme in the views of the better-known Sophists, such as Protagoras, Antiphon (c. 480–411 BCE), and Thrasymachus (flourished late 5th century BCE), is that what is commonly called good and bad or just and unjust does not reflect any objective fact of nature but is rather a matter of social convention. Protagoras is the apparent author of the celebrated epigram summing up this theme: "Man is the measure of all things." Plato represents him as saying, "Whatever things seem just and fine to each city, are just and fine for that city, so long as it thinks them so." Protagoras, like Herodotus, drew a moderate conclusion from his ethical relativism. He argued that, while the particular content of the moral rules may vary, there must be rules of some kind if life is to be tolerable. Thus, Protagoras stated that the foundations of an ethical system needed nothing from the gods or from any special metaphysical realm beyond the ordinary world of the senses.

Thrasymachus appears to have taken a more radical approach—if Plato's portrayal of his views is historically accurate. He explained that the concept of justice means nothing more than obedience to the laws of society, and, since these laws are made by the strongest political group in its own interest, justice represents nothing but the interest of the stronger. This position is often represented by the slogan "Might makes right." Thrasymachus was probably not saying, however, that whatever the mightiest do really is right; he is more likely to have been denying that the distinction between right and wrong has any objective basis. Presumably he would then encourage his pupils to follow their own interests as best they could. He is thus an early representative of moral skepticism and perhaps ethical egoism, the view that the right thing to do is to pursue one's own interest.

It is not surprising that, with ideas of this sort in circulation, other thinkers should react by probing more deeply into ethics to see whether the potentially destructive conclusions of some of the Sophists could be resisted. This reaction produced works that have served ever since as the cornerstone of the entire edifice of Western ethics.

SOCRATES

Socrates, who once observed that "the unexamined life is not worth living," must be regarded as one of the greatest teachers of ethics. Yet, unlike other figures of comparable importance, such as the Buddha or Confucius, he did not tell his audience how they should live. What Socrates taught was a method of inquiry. When the Sophists or their pupils boasted that they knew what justice, piety, temperance, or law was, Socrates would ask them to give an account, which he would then show was entirely inadequate. Because his method of inquiry threatened conventional beliefs, Socrates' enemies contrived to have him put to death on a charge of corrupting the youth of Athens. For those who thought that adherence to the conventional moral code was more important than the cultivation of an inquiring mind, the charge was appropriate. By conventional standards, Socrates was indeed corrupting the youth of Athens, though he himself considered the destruction of beliefs that could not stand up to criticism as a necessary preliminary to the search for true knowledge. In this respect he differed from the Sophists, with their ethical relativism, for he thought that virtue is something that can be known and that the virtuous person is the one who knows what virtue is.

Socrates's method of inquiry was considered so threatening that he was eventually sentenced to death by poison. Hulton Archive/Getty Images

It is therefore not entirely accurate to regard Socrates as contributing a method of inquiry but as having no positive views of his own. He believed that virtue could be known, though he himself did not profess to know it. He also thought that anyone who knows what virtue is will necessarily act virtuously. Those who act badly, therefore, do so only because they are ignorant of, or mistaken about, the real nature of virtue. This belief may seem peculiar today, in large part because it is now common to distinguish between what a person ought to do and what is in his own interest. Once this assumption is made, it is easy to imagine circumstances in which a person knows what he ought to do but proceeds to do something else—what is in his own interests—instead. Indeed, how to provide self-interested (or merely rational) people with motivating reasons for doing what is right has been a major problem for Western ethics. In ancient Greece, however, the distinction between virtue and self-interest was not made—at least not in the clear-cut manner that it is today. The Greeks believed that virtue is good both for the individual and for the community. To be sure, they recognized that living virtuously might not be the best way to prosper financially; but then they did not assume, as people are prone to do today, that material wealth is a major factor in whether a person's life goes well or ill.

PLATO

Socrates' greatest disciple, Plato, accepted the key Socratic beliefs in the objectivity of goodness and in the link between knowing what is good and doing it. He also took over the Socratic method of conducting philosophy, developing the case for his own positions by exposing errors and confusions in the arguments of his opponents. He did this by writing his works as dialogues in which

Socrates is portrayed as engaging in argument with others, usually Sophists. The early dialogues are generally accepted as reasonably accurate accounts of the views of the historical Socrates, but the later ones, written many years after Socrates' death, use the latter as a mouthpiece for ideas and arguments that were in fact original to Plato.

In the most famous of Plato's dialogues, the *Republic*, the character Socrates is challenged by the following example. Suppose a person obtained the legendary ring of Gyges, which has the magical property of rendering the wearer invisible. Would that person still have any reason to behave justly? Behind this challenge lies the suggestion, made by the Sophists and still heard today, that the only reason for acting justly is that one cannot get away with acting unjustly. Plato's response to this challenge is a long argument developing a position that appears to go well beyond anything the historical Socrates asserted. Plato maintained that true knowledge consists not in knowing particular things but in knowing something general that is common to all the particular cases. This view is obviously derived from the way in which Socrates pressed his opponents to go beyond merely describing particular

After his mentor's death, Plato used the Socratic method in dialogue form, usually portraying Socrates in argument with Sophists. Photos.com

acts that are (for example) good, temperate, or just and to give instead a general account of goodness, temperance, or justice. The implication is that one does not know what goodness is unless one can give such a general account. But the question then arises, what is it that one knows when one knows this general idea of goodness? Plato's answer is that one knows the Form of the Good—a perfect, eternal, and changeless entity existing outside space and time, in which particular good things share, or "participate," insofar as they are good.

It has been said that all of Western philosophy consists of footnotes to Plato. Certainly the central issue around which all of Western ethics has revolved can be traced to the debate between the Sophists, who claimed that goodness and justice are relative to the customs of each society—or, worse still, that they are merely a disguise for the interest of the stronger—and the Platonists, who maintained the possibility of knowledge of an objective Form of the Good.

But even if one could know what goodness or justice is, why should one act justly if one could profit by doing the opposite? This is the remaining part of the challenge posed by the tale of the ring of Gyges, and it is still to be answered. For even if one accepts that goodness is something objective, it does not follow that one has a sufficient reason to do what is good. One would have such a reason if it could be shown that goodness or justice leads, at least in the long run, to happiness; as has been seen from the preceding discussion of early ethics in other cultures, this issue is a perennial topic for all who think about ethics.

According to Plato, justice exists in the individual when the three elements of the soul—intellect, emotion, and desire—act in harmony with each other. The unjust person lives in an unsatisfactory state of internal discord, trying always to overcome the discomfort of unsatisfied desire but never achieving anything better than the mere absence of want. The soul of the just person, on the other hand, is harmoniously ordered under the governance of reason, and the just person derives truly satisfying enjoyment from the pursuit of knowledge. Plato remarks that the highest pleasure, in fact, comes from intellectual speculation. He also gives an argument for the belief that the human soul is immortal; therefore, even if a just individual lives in poverty or suffers from illness, the gods will not neglect him in the next life, where he will have the greatest rewards of all. In summary, then, Plato asserts that we should act justly because in doing so we are "at one with ourselves and with the gods."

Today, this may seem like a strange conception of justice and a farfetched view of what it takes to achieve human happiness. Plato does not recommend justice for its own sake, independent of any personal gains one might obtain from being a just person. This is characteristic of Greek ethics, which refused to recognize that there could be an irresolvable conflict between the interest of the individual and the good of the community. Not until the 18th century did a philosopher, Immanuel Kant, forcefully assert the importance of doing what is right simply because it is right, quite apart from self-interested motivation. To be sure, Plato did not hold that the motivation for each and every just act is some personal gain; on the contrary, the person who takes up justice will do what is just because it is just. Nevertheless, he accepted the assumption of his opponents that one could not recommend taking up justice in the first place unless doing so could be shown to be advantageous for oneself as well as for others.

Although many people now think differently about the connection between morality and self-interest, Plato's attempt to argue that those who are just are in the long run happier than those who are unjust has had an enormous influence on Western ethics. Like Plato's views on the objectivity of goodness, the claim that justice and personal happiness are linked has helped to frame the agenda for a debate that continues even today.

ARISTOTLE

Plato founded a school of philosophy in Athens known as the Academy. There Aristotle, Plato's younger contemporary and only rival in terms of influence on the course of Western philosophy, went to study. Aristotle was often fiercely critical of Plato, and his writing is very different in style and content, but the time they spent together is reflected in a considerable amount of common ground. Thus, Aristotle holds with Plato that the life of virtue is rewarding for the virtuous as well as beneficial for the community. Aristotle also agrees that the highest and most satisfying form of human existence involves the exercise of one's rational faculties to the fullest extent. One major point of disagreement concerns Plato's doctrine of Forms, which Aristotle rejected. Thus, Aristotle does not argue that in order to be good one must have knowledge of the Form of the Good.

Aristotle conceived of the universe as a hierarchy in which everything has a function. The highest form of existence is the life of the rational being, and the function of lower beings is to serve this form of life. From this perspective Aristotle defended slavery—because he considered barbarians less rational than Greeks and by nature suited to be "living tools"—and the killing of nonhuman animals for food and clothing. From this perspective also came a view of human nature and an ethical theory derived from it. All living things, Aristotle held, have inherent potentialities, which it is their nature to develop. This is the form of life properly suited to them and constitutes their goal. What, however, is the potentiality of human beings? For Aristotle this question turns out to be equivalent to asking what is distinctive about human beings; and this, of course, is the capacity to reason. The ultimate goal of humans, therefore, is to develop their reasoning powers. When they do this, they are living well, in accordance with their true nature, and they will find this the most rewarding existence possible.

Aristotle thus ends up agreeing with Plato that the life of the intellect is the most rewarding existence, though he was more realistic than Plato in suggesting that such a life would also contain the goods of material prosperity and close friendships. Aristotle's argument for regarding the life of the intellect so highly, however, is different from Plato's, and the difference is significant because Aristotle committed a fallacy that has often been repeated. The fallacy is to assume that whatever capacity distinguishes humans from other beings is, for that very reason, the highest and best of their capacities. Perhaps the ability to reason is the best human capacity, but one cannot be compelled to draw this conclusion from the fact that it is what is most distinctive of the human species.

A broader and still more pervasive fallacy underlies Aristotle's ethics. It is the idea that an investigation of human nature can reveal what one ought to do. For Aristotle, an examination of a knife would reveal that its distinctive capacity is to cut, and from this one could conclude that a good knife is a knife that cuts well. In the same way, an examination of human nature should reveal the distinctive capacity of human beings, and from this one should be able to infer what it is to be a good human being. This line of thought makes sense if one thinks, as Aristotle did, that the universe as a whole has a purpose and that human beings exist as part of such a goal-directed scheme of things, but its error becomes glaring if this view is rejected and human existence is seen as the result of a blind process of evolution. Whereas the distinctive capacity of a knife is a result of the fact that knives are made for a specific purpose—and a good knife is thus one that fulfills this purpose well—human beings, according to modern biology, were not made with any particular purpose in mind. Their nature is the result of random forces of natural selection. Thus, human nature cannot, without further moral premises, determine how human beings ought to live.

Aristotle is also responsible for much later thinking about the virtues one should cultivate. In his most important ethical treatise, the *Nicomachean Ethics*, he sorts through the virtues as they were popularly understood in his day, specifying in each case what is truly virtuous and what is mistakenly thought to be so. Here he applies an idea that later came to be known as the Golden Mean; it is essentially the same as the Buddha's middle path between self-indulgence and self-renunciation. Thus, courage, for example, is the mean between two extremes: one can have a deficiency of it, which is cowardice, or one can have an excess of it, which is foolhardiness. The virtue of friendliness, to give another example, is the mean between obsequiousness and surliness.

Aristotle does not intend the idea of the mean to be applied mechanically in every instance: he says that in the case of the virtue of temperance, or self-restraint, it is easy to find the excess of self-indulgence in the physical pleasures, but the opposite error, insufficient concern for such pleasures, scarcely exists. (The Buddha, who had experienced the ascetic life of renunciation, would not have agreed.) This caution in the application of the idea is just as well, for while it may be a useful device for moral education, the notion of a mean cannot help one to discover new truths about virtue. One can determine the mean only if one already has a notion of what is an excess and what is a defect of the trait in question. But this is not something that can be discovered by a morally neutral inspection of the trait itself: one needs a prior conception of the virtue in order to decide what is excessive and what is defective. Thus, to attempt to use the doctrine of the mean to define the particular virtues would be to travel in a circle.

Aristotle's list of the virtues and vices differs from lists compiled by later Christian thinkers. Although courage, temperance, and liberality are recognized as virtues in both periods, Aristotle also includes a virtue whose Greek name, *megalopsyche*, is sometimes translated as "pride," though it literally means "greatness of soul." This is the characteristic of holding a justified high opinion of oneself. For Christians the corresponding excess, vanity, was a vice, but the corresponding deficiency, humility, was a virtue.

Aristotle's discussion of the virtue of justice has been the starting point of almost all Western accounts. He distinguishes between justice in the distribution of wealth or other goods and justice in reparation, as, for example, in punishing someone for a wrong he has done. The key element of justice, according to Aristotle, is treating like cases alike—an idea that set for later thinkers the task of working out which kinds of similarities (e.g., need, desert, talent) should be relevant. As with the notion of virtue as a mean, Aristotle's conception of justice provides a framework that requires fleshing out before it can be put to use.

Aristotle distinguished between theoretical and practical wisdom. His conception of practical wisdom is significant, for it involves more than merely choosing the best means to whatever ends or goals one may have. The practically wise person also has the right ends. This implies that one's ends are not purely a matter of brute desire or feeling; the right ends are something that can be known and reasoned about. It also gives rise to the problem that faced Socrates: how is it that people can know the difference between good and bad and still choose what is bad? Socrates simply denied that this could happen, saying that those who did not choose the good must, appearances notwithstanding, be ignorant of what the good is. Aristotle said that this view was "plainly at variance with the observed facts," and he offered instead a detailed account of the ways in which one can fail to act on one's knowledge of the good, including the failure that results from lack of self-control and the failure caused by *akrasia*, or weakness of will.

LATER GREEK AND ROMAN ETHICS

In ethics, as in many other fields, the later Greek and Roman periods do not display the same penetrating insight as the Classical period of 5th- and 4th-century Greek civilization. Nevertheless, the two schools of thought that dominated the later periods, Stoicism and Epicureanism, represent important approaches to the question of how one ought to live.

THE STOICS

Stoicism originated in the views of Socrates and Plato, as modified by Zeno of Citium (*c.* 335–*c.* 263 BCE) and then by Chrysippus (*c.* 280–206 BCE). It gradually gained influence in Rome, chiefly through Marcus Tullius Cicero (106–43 BCE) and then later through Seneca the Younger (4 BCE–65 CE). Remarkably, its chief proponents include both a slave, Epictetus (55–*c.* 135 CE), and an emperor, Marcus Aurelius (121–180 CE). This is a fine illustration of the Stoic message that what is important is the pursuit of wisdom and virtue, a quest that is open to all human beings because of their common capacity for reason, no matter what the external circumstances of their lives.

Today, the most common meaning of the word *stoic* is a person who remains unmoved by the sorrows and afflictions that distress the rest of humanity. This is an accurate representation of a Stoic ideal, but it must be placed in the context of a systematic approach to life. Plato held that human passions and physical desires are in need of regulation by reason. The Stoics went farther: they rejected passions altogether as a basis for deciding what is good or bad. Although physical desires cannot simply be abolished, the wise person will appreciate the difference between wanting something and judging it to be good. Only reason can judge the goodness or badness of what is desired. If one is wise, he will identify himself with reason rather than with desire; hence, he will not hope for the satisfaction of physical desires or worry that they might not be satisfied. The Stoic will feel physical pain as others do, but he will know that physical pain leaves the true reasoning self untouched. The only thing that is truly good is to live in a state of wisdom and virtue. In pursuing such a life, one is protected from the play of fortune that afflicts those who aim at physical pleasure or material wealth, for wisdom and virtue are matters of the intellect and under the individual's control. Moreover, if matters become too grim, there is always a way of ending the pain of the physical world. The Stoics were not reluctant to counsel suicide as a means of avoiding otherwise inescapable pain.

Perhaps the most important legacy of Stoicism, however, is its conviction that all human beings share the capacity to reason. This led the Stoics to a fundamental belief in equality, which went beyond the limited Greek conception of equal citizenship. Thus Seneca claimed that the wise man will esteem the community of rational beings far above any particular community in which the accident of birth has placed him, and Marcus Aurelius said that common reason makes all individuals fellow citizens. The belief that the capacity to reason is common to all humans was also important because from it the Stoics drew the implication that there is a universal moral law, which all people are capable of appreciating. The Stoics thus strengthened the tradition that regarded the universality of reason as the basis on which to reject ethical relativism.

THE EPICUREANS

Although the modern use of the term *stoic* accurately represents at least a part of the Stoic philosophy, anyone taking the present-day meaning of *epicure* as a guide to the philosophy of Epicurus (341–270 BCE) would go astray. True, the Epicureans regarded pleasure as the sole ultimate good and pain as the sole evil, and they did regard the more refined pleasures as superior—simply in terms of the quantity and durability of the pleasure they provided—to the coarser pleasures. To portray them as searching for these more refined pleasures by dining at the best restaurants and drinking the finest wines, however, is the reverse of the truth. By refined pleasures, Epicurus meant pleasures of the mind, as opposed to the coarse pleasures of the body. He taught that the highest pleasure obtainable is the pleasure of tranquillity, which is to be obtained by the removal of unsatisfied wants. The way to do this is to eliminate all but the simplest wants; these are then easily satisfied even by those who are not wealthy.

Epicurus developed his position systematically. To determine whether something is good, he would ask if it increased pleasure or reduced pain. If it did, it was good as a means; if it did not, it was not good at all. Thus, justice was good but merely as an expedient arrangement to prevent mutual harm. Why not then commit injustice when we can get away with it? Only because, Epicurus says, the perpetual dread of discovery will cause painful anxiety. Epicurus also exalted friendship, and the Epicureans were famous for the warmth of their personal relationships; but, again, they proclaimed that friendship is good only because of its tendency to create pleasure.

Both Stoic and Epicurean ethics were precursors of later trends in Western ethics: the Stoics of the modern belief in equality and the Epicureans of a utilitarian ethics based on pleasure. The development of these ethical positions, however, was dramatically affected by the spreading from the East of a new religion, Christianity, that was rooted in a Jewish conception of ethics as obedience to a divine authority. With the conversion of Emperor

Epicurus commended friendship because of the joy it produces. Jupiterimages/ Brand X Pictures/Getty Images

Constantine I (*c.* 280–337 CE) to Christianity by the year 313, the older schools of philosophy lost their sway over the thinking of the Roman Empire.

ETHICS IN THE NEW TESTAMENT

The apostle Matthew reports Jesus as having said, in the Sermon on the Mount, that he came not to destroy the law of the prophets but to fulfill it. Indeed, when Jesus is regarded as a teacher of ethics, it is clear that he was more a reformer of the Hebrew tradition than a radical innovator. The Hebrew tradition had a tendency to place great emphasis on compliance with the letter of the law; the Gospel accounts of Jesus portray him as preaching against this "righteousness of the scribes and Pharisees," championing the spirit of the law rather than the letter. This spirit he characterized as one of love, for God and for one's neighbour. But since he was not proposing that the old teachings be discarded, he saw no need to develop a comprehensive ethical system. Christianity thus never really broke with the Jewish conception of morality as a matter of divine law to be discovered by reading and interpreting the word of God as revealed in the Scriptures.

This conception of morality had important consequences for the future development of Western ethics. The Greeks and Romans—and indeed thinkers such as Confucius—did not conceive of a distinctively moral realm of conduct. For them, everything that one did was a matter of practical reasoning, in which one could do either well or poorly. In the more legalistic Judeo-Christian view, however, falling short of what the moral law requires was a much more serious matter than, say, failing to do the household budgets correctly. This distinction between the moral and the nonmoral realms now affects every question in Western ethics, including the way the questions themselves are framed.

Another consequence of the retention of the basically legalistic stance of Jewish ethics was that from the beginning Christian ethics had to deal with the question of how to judge the person who breaks the law with good motives or keeps it with bad motives. The latter half of this question was particularly acute, because the Gospels describe Jesus as repeatedly warning of a coming resurrection of

When viewed in light of his ethical teaching, Jesus was a reformer of Hebrew convention. Rischgitz/Hulton Archive/Getty Images

the dead at which time all would be judged and punished or rewarded according to their sins and virtues in this life. The punishments and rewards were weighty enough to motivate anyone who took this message seriously, and the warning was given added emphasis by the fact that the resurrection was not going to be long in coming. (Jesus said that it would take place during the lifetime of some of those listening to him.) This is therefore an ethics that invokes external sanctions as a reason for doing what is right. At the same time, it is an ethics that places love above mere literal compliance with the law. These two aspects do not sit easily together. Can one bring oneself to love God and neighbour in order to be rewarded with eternal happiness in another life?

The fact that Jesus and the apostle Paul too believed in the imminence of the Second Coming led them to suggest ways of living that were scarcely feasible on any other assumption: taking no thought for the morrow, turning the other cheek, and giving away all one has. Even Paul's preference for celibacy rather than marriage and his grudging acceptance of the latter on the assumption that "it is better to marry than to burn" makes some sense, once one grasps that he was proposing ethical standards for what he thought would be the last generation on earth. When the expected event did not occur and Christianity became the official religion of the vast and embattled Roman Empire, Christian leaders were faced with the awkward task of reinterpreting these injunctions in a manner more suited for a continuing society.

The new Christian ethical standards did lead to some changes in Roman morality. Perhaps the most vital change was a new sense of the equal moral status of all human beings. The Stoics had been the first to elaborate this conception, grounding equality on the common capacity to reason. For Christians, humans are equal because they are all potentially immortal and equally precious in the sight of God. This caused Christians to condemn a wide variety of practices that had been accepted by both Greek and Roman moralists, including many related to the taking of innocent human life: from the earliest days Christian leaders condemned abortion, infanticide, and suicide. Even killing in war was at first regarded as wrong, and soldiers who had converted to Christianity refused to continue to bear arms. Once the empire became Christian, however, this was one of the inconvenient ideas that had to yield. Despite what Jesus had said about turning the other cheek, church leaders declared that killing in a "just war" was not a sin. The Christian condemnation of killing in gladiatorial games, on the other hand, had a more permanent effect. Finally, but perhaps most important, while Christian emperors continued to uphold the legality of slavery, the Christian church accepted slaves as equals, admitted them to its ceremonies, and regarded the granting of freedom to slaves as a virtuous, if not obligatory, act. This moral pressure led over several hundred years to the gradual disappearance of slavery in Europe.

The Christian contribution to improving the position of slaves can also be linked with the distinctively Christian list of virtues. Some of the virtues described by Aristotle—for example, greatness of soul—are quite contrary in spirit to Christian virtues such as humility. In general it can be said that, whereas the Greeks and Romans prized independence, self-reliance, magnanimity, and worldly success, Christians emphasized meekness, obedience, patience, and resignation. As the Greeks and Romans conceived virtue, a virtuous slave was almost a contradiction in terms; for Christians, however, there was nothing in the state of slavery that was incompatible with the highest moral character.

Moral Theology

Moral theology, also called Christian ethics, is the discipline concerned with identifying and elucidating principles for judging the moral quality of human behaviour in the light of Christian revelation. It is distinguished from the philosophical discipline of ethics, which relies upon the authority of reason and which can only call upon rational sanctions for moral failure. Moral theology appeals to the authority of revelation, specifically as found in the preaching and activity of Jesus Christ.

Moral teaching in Christian communities has varied in the different eras, regions, and confessional traditions in which Christianity has been professed. The Roman Catholic tradition has been inclined to emphasize the mediating role of ecclesiastical institutions in its approach to the moral authority of revelation. Protestant churches have often put great emphasis on the direct, or immediate, moral responsibility of the individual before God. The influence of the spiritual director for the moral welfare of the individual Christian has been a significant aspect of Eastern Christianity.

The significance of the relation of moral teaching to divine revelation lies in the problem of determining the nature of the particular "highest good" that characterizes any ethical system. Without such a determination of the nature of this good, one could easily have the impression that morality is simply obedience to a set of rules or laws the observance of which has been labeled, more or less arbitrarily, "good." In the light of revelation, sin is seen as a deterioration of the fundamental disposition of a person toward God, rather than as a breaking of rules or laws. Virtue is viewed as the habitual capacity of a person to respond freely and consciously to situations in a manner that reflects and intensifies his conformity to Jesus Christ.

The diverse approaches to moral theology through the centuries have varied greatly in their recourse to logical reasoning and in the degree of their acceptance of general moral principles that are considered universally applicable. Contemporary moral theology must confront a variety of problems, including the scope of individual responsibility in large corporate institutions, the effects of human activities on the natural environment, the demands of social justice, the developments in genetics and other biological sciences, and the use of sophisticated technology in warfare.

SAINT AUGUSTINE

At its beginning, Christianity had a set of scriptures incorporating many moral injunctions, but it did not have a moral philosophy. The first serious attempt to provide such a philosophy was made by St. Augustine of Hippo (354–430). Augustine was acquainted with a version of Plato's philosophy, and he developed the Platonic idea of the rational soul into a Christian view in which humans are essentially souls, using their bodies as a means to achieve their spiritual ends. The ultimate objective remains happiness, as in Greek ethics, but Augustine conceived of happiness as consisting of the union of the soul with God after the body has died. It was through Augustine, therefore, that Christianity received the Platonic theme of the relative inferiority of bodily pleasures. There was, to be sure, a fundamental difference: whereas for Plato bodily pleasures were inferior in comparison with the pleasures of philosophical contemplation in this world, for Christians they were inferior to the pleasures of spiritual existence in the next world. Moreover, Christians came to regard bodily pleasures not merely as inferior but also as a positive threat to the achievement of spiritual bliss.

It was also important that Augustine could not accept the view, common to so many Greek and Roman philosophers, that philosophical reasoning was the means to achieving wisdom and happiness. For a Christian, of course, wisdom and happiness can be had only through love of God and faith in Jesus Christ as the Saviour. The result was to be, for many centuries, a rejection of the use of unfettered reasoning in ethics.

Augustine was aware of the tension between the dual Christian motivations of love of God and neighbour on the one hand and reward and punishment in the afterlife on the other. He came down firmly on the side of love, insisting that those who keep the moral law through fear of punishment are not really keeping it at all. But it is not ordinary human love, either, that suffices as a motivation for true Christian living. Augustine believed that all human beings bear the burden of Adam's original sin and so are incapable of redeeming themselves by their own efforts. Only the unmerited grace of God makes possible obedience to the "first greatest commandment" of loving God, and without it one cannot fulfill the moral law. This view made a clear-cut distinction between Christians and pagan moralists, no matter how humble and pure the latter might be; only the former could be saved, because only they could receive the blessing of divine grace. But this gain, as Augustine saw it, was purchased at the cost of denying that humans are free to choose good or evil. Only Adam had this choice: he chose for all humanity, and he chose evil.

CHAPTER 3

The Middle Ages to the Protestant Reformation

A fter Augustine there were no major developments in ethics in the West until the rise of Scholasticism in the 12th and 13th centuries. Among the first significant works written during this time was a treatise on ethics by the French philosopher and theologian Peter Abelard (1079–1142). His importance in ethical theory lies in his emphasis on intentions. Abelard maintained, for example, that the sin of sexual wrongdoing consists not in the act of illicit sexual intercourse, nor even in the desire for it, but in mentally consenting to that desire. In this he was far more modern than Augustine and more thoughtful than those who even today assert that the mere desire for what is wrong is as wrong as the act itself. Abelard recognized that there is a problem in holding a person morally responsible for the mere existence of physical desires. His ingenious solution was taken up by later medieval writers, and traces of it can still be found in modern discussions of moral responsibility.

SAINT THOMAS AQUINAS AND THE SCHOLASTICS

Aristotle's ethical writings were not known to scholars in western Europe during Abelard's time. Latin translations became available only in the first half of the

Peter Abelard questioned the validity of holding one accountable for the presence of physical desires. Hulton Archive/Getty Images

13th century, and the rediscovery of Aristotle dominated later medieval philosophy. Nowhere is his influence more marked than in the thought of St. Thomas Aquinas (1225–74), who is often regarded as the greatest of the Scholastic philosophers and is undoubtedly the most influential, since his teachings became the semiofficial philosophy of the Roman Catholic Church. Such is the respect in which Aquinas held Aristotle that he referred to him simply as "The Philosopher." Indeed, it is not too far from the truth to say that the chief aim of Aquinas's work was to reconcile Aristotle's views with Christian doctrine.

Aquinas took from Aristotle the notion of an ultimate end, or goal—a summum bonum—at which all human action is directed; and, like Aristotle, he conceived of this end as necessarily connected with happiness. This conception was Christianized, however, by the idea that happiness is to be found in the love of God. Thus, a person seeks to know God but cannot fully succeed in doing so in his life on earth. The reward of heaven, where one can know God, is available only to those who merit it, though even then it is given by God's grace rather than obtained by right. Short of heaven, a person can experience only a more limited form of happiness through a life of virtue and friendship, much as Aristotle had recommended.

The blend of Aristotle's teachings and Christianity is also evident in Aquinas's views about right and wrong and about how one comes to know the difference between the two. Aquinas is often described as advocating a "natural law" ethic, but this term is easily misunderstood. The natural law to which Aquinas referred does not require a legislator, any more than do the laws of nature that govern the motions of the planets. An even more common mistake is to imagine that this conception of natural law relies on contrasting what is natural with what is artificial. Aquinas's theory of the basis of right and wrong developed rather as an alternative to the view that morality is determined simply by the arbitrary will of God. Instead of conceiving of right and wrong in this manner as something fundamentally unrelated to human goals and purposes, Aquinas viewed morality as deriving from human nature and the activities that are objectively suited to it.

Aquinas combined the ethical teachings of Aristotle and Christianity in his views about right and wrong and how we can tell the difference between them. Hulton Archive/ Getty Images

It is a consequence of this natural law ethics that the difference between right and wrong can be appreciated by the use of reason and reflection on experience. Although Christian revelation may supplement this knowledge in some respects, even pagan philosophers such as Aristotle could understand the essentials of virtuous living. One is, however, likely to err when applying these general principles to the particular cases one confronts in everyday life. Corrupt customs and poor moral education may obscure the conclusions of natural reason. Hence, societies must enact laws of their own to supplement natural law and, where necessary, to coerce those who, because of their own imperfections, are liable to do what is wrong and socially destructive.

It follows too that virtue and human flourishing are linked. When one does what is right, he does what is objectively suited to his true nature. Thus, the promise of heaven is no mere external sanction, rewarding actions to which one would otherwise be indifferent or that may even be against one's interest. On the contrary, Aquinas wrote that "God is not offended by us except by what we do against our own good." Reward and punishment in the afterlife reinforce a moral law that all humans, Christian as well as pagan, have adequate prior reasons for following.

In arguing for his views, Aquinas was always concerned to show that he had on his side the authority of the Scriptures or the Church Fathers (the great bishops and teachers of the early centuries of Christianity), but the substance of his ethical system is to a remarkable degree based on reason rather than revelation. This is strong testimony to the power of Aristotle's example. Nonetheless, Aquinas absorbed the weaknesses as well as the strengths of the Aristotelian system. In particular, his attempt to base right and wrong on human nature invites the objection that one cannot presuppose human nature to be good. Aquinas might reply that it is good because God made it so, but this merely pushes back one step the issue of the basis of good and bad: did God make human nature good in accordance with some independent standard of goodness, or would any human nature made by God be good? If one gives the former answer, then one needs an account of the independent standard of goodness. Because this standard cannot be based on human nature (for then the argument would be circular), it is not clear what account Aquinas could offer. If one maintains that any human nature made by God would be good, then one must accept that, if God had made human nature such that humans flourish and achieve happiness by torturing the weak and helpless, that would have been what humans should do in order to live virtuously.

Something resembling this second option—but without the intermediate step of an appeal to human nature—was the position taken by the last of the great Scholastic philosophers, William of Ockham (*c.* 1285–1347/49). Ockham boldly broke with much that had been taken for granted by his immediate predecessors. Fundamental to his approach was his rejection of the central Aristotelian idea that all things have an ultimate end toward which they naturally tend. He therefore also spurned Aquinas's attempt to base morality on human nature and with it the idea that goodness is closely connected with happiness, which is the ultimate end of human beings. Ockham was thus led to a position that contrasted starkly with almost all previous ethical doctrines in the West. Ockham denied all standards of good and evil that are independent of God's will. What God wills is good; what God condemns is evil. That is all there is to say about the matter. This position is sometimes called a divine approbation theory, because it defines *good* as whatever is approved by God. It follows from such a position that it is meaningless to describe God himself as good. It also follows that if God had willed humans to torture children, it would be good to do so. As for the actual content of God's will, according to Ockham, that is not a subject for philosophy but rather a matter for revelation and faith.

The rigour and consistency of Ockham's philosophy made it for a time one of the leading schools of Scholastic thought, but eventually it was the philosophy of Aquinas that prevailed in the Roman Catholic Church. After the Reformation, however, Ockham's view was influential among Protestant theologians. Meanwhile, it hastened the decline of Scholastic moral philosophy, because it effectively removed ethics from the sphere of reason.

Natural Law

Natural law is a system of rights or justice held to be common to all humans and derived from nature rather than from the rules of society, or positive law.

Philosophers and legal theorists have disagreed over the meaning of natural law and its relation to positive law. Aristotle held that what was "just by nature" was not always the same as what was "just by law," that there was a natural justice valid everywhere with the same force and "not existing by people's thinking this or that," and that appeal could be made to it from positive law. In contrast, the Stoics conceived of an entirely egalitarian law of nature in conformity with the logos (reason) inherent in the universe.

St. Thomas Aquinas propounded an influential systematization, maintaining that, though the eternal law of divine reason is known in part not only by revelation but also by the operations of reason. The law of nature thus comprises those precepts that humankind is able to formulate: the preservation of one's own good, the fulfillment of "those inclinations which nature has taught to all animals," and the pursuit of the knowledge of God.

In an epoch-making appeal, the Dutch jurist Hugo Grotius (1583–1645) claimed that nations are subject to natural law. A few years later Thomas Hobbes (1588–1679), starting from the assumption of a savage "state of nature" in which each person was at war with every other, defined a law of nature as "a precept or general rule found out by reason, by which a man is forbidden to do that which is destructive of his life." He then enumerated the elementary rules on which peace and society could be established. John Locke (1632–1704) departed from Hobbesian pessimism to the extent of describing the state of nature as a state of society, with free and equal men already observing the natural law. In France Charles-Louis de Secondat Montesquieu

(1689–1755) argued that natural laws were presocial and superior to those of religion and the state, and Jean-Jacques Rousseau (1712–78) postulated a savage who was virtuous in isolation and actuated by two principles "prior to reason": self-preservation and compassion.

The confidence in appeals to natural law displayed by 17th- and 18th-century philosophers and the authors of the American Declaration of Independence evaporated in the early 19th century. The philosophy of Immanuel Kant (1724–1804), as well as the utilitarianism of Jeremy Bentham (1748–1832), served to weaken the belief that nature could be the source of moral or legal norms. In the mid-20th century, however, there was a revival of interest in natural law, sparked by the widespread belief that the Nazi regime in Germany (1933–45) had been essentially lawless. As in previous centuries, the need to challenge the unjust laws of particular states inspired the desire to invoke rules of right and justice held to be natural rather than merely conventional.

THE RENAISSANCE AND THE REFORMATION

The revival of Classical learning and culture that began in 15th-century Italy and then slowly spread throughout Europe did not give immediate birth to any major new ethical theories. Its significance for ethics lies, rather, in a change of focus. For the first time since the conversion of the Roman Empire to Christianity, God ceased to be the chief object of philosophical interest: the main theme of philosophical thinking was not religion but humanity—the powers, freedom, and accomplishments of human beings. This does not mean that there was a sudden conversion to atheism. Most Renaissance thinkers remained Christian, and they still considered human beings as being somehow midway between the beasts and the angels. Yet, even this middle position meant that humans were special.

It meant, too, a new conception of human dignity and of the importance of the individual.

NICCOLÒ MACHIAVELLI

Although the Renaissance did not produce any outstanding moral philosophers, there is one writer whose work is of some importance in the history of ethics: Niccolò Machiavelli (1469–1527). His book *The Prince* (1513) offered advice to rulers as to what they must do to achieve their aims and secure their power. Its significance for ethics lies precisely in the fact that Machiavelli's advice ignores the usual ethical rules: "It is necessary for a prince, who wishes to maintain himself, to learn how not to be good, and to use this knowledge and not use it, according to the necessities of the case." There had not been so frank a rejection of morality since the Greek Sophists. So startling is the cynicism of Machiavelli's advice that it has been suggested that *The Prince* was an attempt to satirize the conduct of the princely rulers of Renaissance Italy. It may be more accurate, however, to view Machiavelli as an early political scientist, concerned only with setting out what human beings are like and how power is maintained, with no intention of passing moral judgment on the state of affairs described. In any case, *The Prince* gained instant notoriety, and Machiavelli's name became synonymous with political cynicism and deviousness. Despite the chorus of condemnation, the work led to a sharper appreciation of the difference between the lofty ethical systems of philosophers and the practical realities of political life.

THE FIRST PROTESTANTS

It was left to the English philosopher and political theorist Thomas Hobbes (1588–1679) to take up the challenge of

Niccolò Machiavelli's book The Prince *offered advice to Italian princes and highlighted the disparities between philosophy and real life.* Time & Life Pictures/Getty Images

constructing an ethical system on the basis of so unflattering a view of human nature. Between Machiavelli and Hobbes, however, there occurred the traumatic breakup of Western Christendom known as the Reformation. Reacting against the worldly immorality apparent in the Renaissance church, Martin Luther (1483–1546), John Calvin (1509–64), and other leaders of the new Protestantism sought to return to the pure early Christianity of the Scriptures, especially as reflected in the teachings of Paul and of the Church Fathers,

Augustine foremost among them. They were contemptuous of Aristotle (Luther called him a "buffoon") and of non-Christian philosophers in general. Luther's standard of right and wrong was whatever God commands. Like William of Ockham, Luther insisted that the commands of God cannot be justified by any independent standard of goodness: good simply means what God commands. Luther did not believe that these commands would be designed by God to satisfy human desires, because he was convinced that human desires are totally corrupt. In fact, he thought that human nature itself is totally corrupt. In any case, Luther insisted that one does not earn salvation by good works; one is justified by faith in Christ and receives salvation through divine grace.

It is apparent that if these premises are accepted, there is little scope for human reason in ethics. As a result, no moral philosophy has ever had the kind of close association with any Protestant church that, for example, the philosophy of Aquinas has had with Roman Catholicism. Yet, because Protestants emphasized the capacity of the individual to read and understand the Gospels without first receiving the authoritative interpretation of the church, the ultimate outcome of the Reformation was a greater freedom to read and write independently of the church hierarchy. This development made possible a new era of ethical thought.

From this time, too, distinctively national traditions of moral philosophy began to emerge. The British tradition, in particular, developed largely independently of ethics on the European continent. Accordingly, the present discussion will follow this tradition from the 17th through the 19th century—conventionally regarded as the modern period of Western philosophy—before returning to consider the concurrent but importantly different line of development in continental Europe.

CHAPTER 4

THE 17TH TO THE 19TH CENTURY: BRITAIN

In Britain the most influential ethical thinkers of the modern period were Thomas Hobbes; the moral intuitionists Ralph Cudworth (1617–88), Henry More (1614–87), Samuel Clarke (1675–1729), Richard Price (1723–91), and Thomas Reid (1710–96); the moral sense theorists Anthony Ashley Cooper, the 3rd earl of Shaftesbury (1671–1713), Joseph Butler (1692–1752), Francis Hutcheson (1694–1746), and David Hume (1711–76); and the utilitarians, especially William Paley (1743–1805), Jeremy Bentham (1748–1832), John Stuart Mill (1806–73), and Henry Sidgwick (1838–1900).

THOMAS HOBBES

Thomas Hobbes is an outstanding example of the independence of mind that became possible in Protestant countries after the Reformation. To be sure, God does play an honourable role in Hobbes's philosophy, but it is a dispensable role. The philosophical edifice he constructed stands on its own foundations; God merely crowns the apex. Hobbes was the equal of the Greek philosophers in his readiness to develop an ethical position based only on the facts of human nature and the circumstances in which humans live, and he surpassed even Plato and Aristotle in the extent to which

In the philosophy of Thomas Hobbes God plays only a minor role. Time & Life Pictures/Getty Images

he sought to do this by systematic deduction from clearly stated premises.

Hobbes started with a severe view of human nature: all of the voluntary acts of human beings are aimed at pleasure or self-preservation. This position is known as psychological hedonism, because it asserts that the fundamental motivation of all human action is the desire for pleasure. Like later psychological hedonists, Hobbes was confronted with the objection that people often seem to act altruistically. According to a story told about him, Hobbes was once seen giving alms to a beggar outside St. Paul's Cathedral. A clergyman sought to score a point by asking Hobbes whether he would have given the money had Christ not urged giving to the poor. Hobbes replied that he gave the money because it pleased him to see the poor man pleased. The reply reveals the dilemma that always faces those who propose startling new explanations for human actions: either the theory is flagrantly at odds with how people really behave, or else it must be broadened or diluted to such an extent that it loses much of what made it so shocking in the first place.

Hobbes's definition of *good* is equally devoid of religious or metaphysical assumptions. A thing is good, according to him, if it is "the object of any man's appetite or desire." He insisted that the term must be used in relation to a person—nothing is simply good in itself, independently of any person who may desire it. Hobbes may therefore be considered an ethical subjectivist. Thus, if one were to say of the incident just described, "What Hobbes did was good," one's statement would not be objectively true or false. It would be true for the poor man, and, if Hobbes's reply was accurate, it would also be true for Hobbes. But if a second poor person, for instance, was jealous of the success of the first, that person could quite properly say that the statement is false for him.

Remarkably, this unpromising picture of self-interested individuals who have no notion of good apart from their own desires served as the foundation of Hobbes's account of justice and morality in his masterpiece, *Leviathan* (1651). Starting with the premises that humans are self-interested and that the world does not provide for all their needs, Hobbes argued that in the hypothetical state of nature, before the existence of civil society, there was competition between men for wealth, security, and glory. What would ensue in such a state is Hobbes's famous "war of all against all," in which there could be no industry, commerce, or civilization, and in which the human life would be "solitary, poor, nasty, brutish, and short." The struggle would occur because each individual would rationally pursue his own interests, but the outcome would be in no one's interests.

How can this disastrous situation be avoided? Not by an appeal to morality or justice; in the state of nature these ideas have no meaning. Yet, everyone wishes to survive, and everyone can reason. Reason leads people to seek peace if it is attainable but to continue to use all the means of war if it is not. How is peace to be obtained? Only by a means of a social contract, in which each person agrees to give up his right to attack others in return for the same concession from everyone else.

But how is the social contract to come about? Hobbes is not under the illusion that the mere making of a promise in a contract will carry any weight. Because everyone is rational and self-interested, no one will keep his promise unless it is in his interest to do so. Therefore, in order for the contract to work, there must be some means of enforcing it. To do this, everyone must hand over his powers to some other person or group of persons who will punish anyone who breaches the contract. This person or group of persons Hobbes calls the "sovereign." The sovereign may be a monarch, an elected legislature, or almost any other form of political authority; the essence of sovereignty is only the possession of sufficient power to keep the peace by punishing those who would break it. When such a sovereign—the Leviathan—exists, justice becomes possible because agreements and promises are necessarily kept. At the same time, each person has adequate reason to behave justly, for the sovereign will ensure that those who do not keep their agreements are suitably punished.

Hobbes witnessed the turbulence and near anarchy of the English Civil Wars (1642–51) and was keenly aware of the dangers caused by disputed sovereignty. His solution was to insist that sovereignty must not be divided. Because the sovereign is appointed to enforce the social contract that is fundamental to peace, it is rational to resist the sovereign only if it directly threatens one's life. Hobbes was, in effect, a supporter of absolute sovereignty, and this has been the focus of much political discussion of his ideas. His significance for ethics, however, lies rather in his success in dealing with the subject independently of theology and of quasi-Aristotelian doctrines, such as the view that the world is designed for the benefit of human beings. With this achievement, Hobbes brought ethics into the modern era.

Social Contract

In political philosophy a social contract is an actual or hypothetical compact, or agreement, between the ruled and their rulers, defining the rights and duties of each. In primeval times, according to the theory, individuals were born into an anarchic state of nature, which was happy or unhappy according to the particular version. They then, by exercising natural reason, formed a society (and a government) by means of a contract among themselves.

Although similar ideas can be traced back to the Greek Sophists, social-contract theories had their greatest currency in the 17th and 18th centuries and are associated with such names as Thomas Hobbes, John Locke, and Jean-Jacques Rousseau. What distinguished these theories of political obligation from other doctrines of the period was their attempt to justify political authority on grounds of individual self-interest and rational consent. They attempted to demonstrate the value and purposes of organized government by comparing the advantages of civil society with the disadvantages of the state of nature, a hypothetical condition characterized by a complete absence of governmental authority. The purpose of this comparison was to show why and under what conditions government is useful and ought therefore to be accepted by all reasonable people as a voluntary obligation. These conclusions were then reduced to the form of a social contract, from which it was supposed that all the essential rights and duties of citizens could be logically deduced.

Theories of the social contract differed according to their purpose: some were designed to justify the power of the sovereign; on the other hand, some were intended to safeguard the individual from oppression by an all-too-powerful sovereign.

The more perceptive social-contract theorists, including Hobbes, invariably recognized that their concepts of the social contract and the state of nature were unhistorical and that they could be justified only as hypotheses useful for the clarification of timeless political problems.

THE EARLY INTUITIONISTS

There was, of course, immediate opposition to Hobbes's views. Ralph Cudworth, one of a group of philosophers and theologians known as the Cambridge Platonists, defended a position in some respects similar to that of Plato. That is to say, Cudworth believed that the distinction between good and evil does not lie in human desires but is something objective that can be known by reason, just as the truths of mathematics can be known by reason. Cudworth was thus a forerunner of what has since come to be called ethical intuitionism, the view that there are objective moral truths that can be known by a kind of rational intuition. This view was to attract the support of a series of distinguished thinkers through the early 20th century, when it became for a time the dominant view in British academic philosophy.

Henry More, another leading member of the Cambridge Platonists, attempted to give effect to the comparison between mathematics and morality by formulating moral axioms that could be recognized as self-evidently true. In marked contrast to Hobbes, More included an "axiom of benevolence": "If it be good that one man should be supplied with the means of living well and happily, it is mathematically certain that it is doubly good that two should be so supplied, and so on." Here, More was attempting to build on something that Hobbes himself accepted—namely, the desire of each individual

Ralph Cudworth proposed the idea that good and evil are objective and knowable through reason, as are the truths of mathematics. Shutterstock.com

to be supplied with the means of living well. More, however, wanted to enlist reason to show how one could move beyond this narrow egoism to a universal benevolence. There are traces of this line of thought in the Stoics, but it was More who introduced it into British ethical thinking, wherein it is still very much alive.

Samuel Clarke, the next major intuitionist, accepted More's axiom of benevolence in slightly different words. He was also responsible for a "principle of equity," which, though derived from the Golden Rule so widespread in ancient ethics, was formulated with a new precision: "Whatever I judge reasonable or unreasonable for another to do for me, that by the same judgment I declare reasonable or unreasonable that I in the like case should do for him." As for the means by which these moral truths are known, Clarke accepted Cudworth's and More's analogy with truths of mathematics and added the idea that what human reason discerns is a certain "fitness or unfitness" about the relationship between circumstances and actions. The right action in a given set of circumstances is the fitting one; the wrong action is unfitting. This is something known intuitively and is self-evident.

Clarke's notion of fitness is obscure, but intuitionism faces a still more serious problem that has always been a barrier to its acceptance. Suppose that it is possible to discern through reason that it would be wrong to deceive a person for profit. How does the discerning of this moral truth provide one with a motive sufficient to override the desire for profit? The position of the intuitionist divorces one's moral knowledge from the psychological forces that motivate human action.

The punitive power of Hobbes's sovereign is, of course, one way to provide sufficient motivation for obedience to the social contract and to the laws decreed by the sovereign as necessary for the peaceful functioning of society. The intuitionists, however, wanted to show that morality is objective and holds in all circumstances, whether there is a sovereign or not. Reward and punishment in the afterlife, administered by an all-powerful God, would provide a more universal motive; and some intuitionists, such as Clarke, did make use of this divine sanction. Other thinkers, however, wanted to show that it is reasonable to do what is good independently of the threats of any external power, human or divine. This desire lay behind the development of the major alternative to intuitionism in 17th- and 18th-century British moral philosophy: moral sense theory. The debate between the intuitionists and the moral sense theorists aired for the first time the major issue in what is still the central debate in moral philosophy: is morality based on reason or on feelings?

THE MORAL SENSE SCHOOL

The term *moral sense* was first used by Anthony Ashley Cooper, better known as the 3rd earl of Shaftesbury, whose writings reflect the optimistic tone both of the school of thought he founded and of so much of the philosophy of the 18th-century Enlightenment. Shaftesbury believed that Hobbes had erred by presenting a one-sided picture of human nature. Selfishness is not the only natural passion. There are also natural feelings such as benevolence, generosity, sympathy, gratitude, and so on. These feelings give one an "affection for virtue"—what Shaftesbury called a moral sense—which creates a natural harmony between virtue and self-interest. Shaftesbury was, of course, realistic enough to acknowledge that there are also contrary desires and that not all people are virtuous all of the time. Virtue could, however, be recommended because—and

Anthony Ashley Cooper, popularly known as the 3rd Earl Of Shaftesbury, first coined the term moral sense. Archive Photos/Getty Images

here Shaftesbury drew upon a theme of Greek ethics—
the pleasures of virtue are superior to the pleasures of vice.

JOSEPH BUTLER

Joseph Butler, a bishop of the Church of England,
developed Shaftesbury's position in two ways. He
strengthened the case for a harmony between morality
and enlightened self-interest by claiming that happiness occurs as a by-product of the satisfaction of desires
for things other than happiness itself. Those who aim
directly at happiness do not find it; those whose goals lie
elsewhere are more likely to achieve happiness as well.
Butler was not doubting the reasonableness of pursuing
one's own happiness as an ultimate aim. Indeed, he went
so far as to say that "when we sit down in a cool hour,
we can neither justify to ourselves this or any other
pursuit, till we are convinced that it will be for our happiness, or at least not contrary to it." He held, however,
that direct and simple egoism is a self-defeating strategy. Egoists will do better for themselves by adopting
immediate goals other than their own interests and living their everyday lives in accordance with these more
immediate goals.

Butler's second addition to Shaftesbury's account was
the idea of conscience. This he conceived as a second natural guide to conduct, alongside enlightened self-interest.
Butler believed that there is no inconsistency between the
two; he admitted, however, that skeptics may doubt "the
happy tendency of virtue," and for them conscience can
serve as an authoritative guide. Just what reason skeptics
would have to follow conscience, if they believe its guidance to be contrary to their own happiness, is something
that Butler did not adequately explain. Nevertheless, his
introduction of conscience as an independent source of

moral reasoning reflects an important difference between ancient and modern ethical thinking. The Greek and Roman philosophers would have had no difficulty in accepting everything Butler said about the pursuit of happiness, but they would not have understood his idea of another independent source of rational guidance. Although Butler insisted that the two operate in harmony, this was for him a fortunate fact about the world and not a necessary principle of reason. Thus, his recognition of conscience opened the way for later formulations

Conscience

Conscience is a personal sense of the moral content of one's own conduct, intentions, or character with regard to a feeling of obligation to do right or be good. Conscience, usually informed by acculturation and instruction, is thus generally understood to give intuitively authoritative judgments regarding the moral quality of single actions.

In some belief systems, conscience is regarded as the voice of God and therefore a completely reliable guide of conduct: among the Hindus it is considered "the invisible God who dwells within us." Among Western religious groups, the Society of Friends (or Quakers) places particular emphasis on the role of conscience in apprehending and responding through conduct to the "Inner Light" of God.

Outside the context of religion, philosophers, social scientists, and psychologists have sought to understand conscience in both its individual and universal aspects. The view that holds conscience to be an innate, intuitive faculty determining the perception of right and wrong is called intuitionism. The view that holds conscience to be a cumulative and subjective inference from past experience giving direction to future conduct is called empiricism. Another explanation of conscience was put forth in the 20th century by Sigmund Freud in his postulation of the "superego." According to Freud, the superego is a major element of personality that is formed by the child's incorporation of moral values through parental approval or punishment. The resulting internalized set of prohibitions, condemnations, and inhibitions is that part of the superego known as conscience.

of a universal principle of conduct at odds with the path indicated by even the most enlightened forms of self-interested reasoning.

FRANCIS HUTCHESON AND DAVID HUME

The moral sense school reached its fullest development in the works of two Scottish philosophers, Francis Hutcheson and David Hume. Hutcheson was concerned with showing, against the intuitionists, that moral judgment cannot be based on reason and therefore must be a matter of whether an action is "amiable or disagreeable" to one's moral sense. Like Butler's notion of conscience, Hutcheson's moral sense does not find pleasing only, or even predominantly, those actions that are in one's own interest. On the contrary, Hutcheson conceived moral sense as based on a disinterested benevolence. This led him to state, as the ultimate criterion of the goodness of an action, a principle that was to serve as the basis for the utilitarian reformers: "That action is best which procures the greatest happiness for the greatest numbers."

Hume, like Hutcheson, held that reason cannot be the basis of morality. His chief ground for this conclusion was that morality is essentially practical: there is no point in judging something good if the judgment does not incline one to act accordingly. Reason alone, however, Hume regarded as "the slave of the passions." Reason can show people how best to achieve their ends, but it cannot determine what those ends should be; it is incapable of moving one to action except in accordance with some prior want or desire. Hence, reason cannot give rise to moral judgments.

This is an important argument that is still employed in the debate between those who believe that morality is based on reason and those who base it instead on emotion or feelings. Hume's conclusion certainly follows from his premises. Can either premise be denied? Intuitionists such as Cudworth and Clarke maintained that reason can lead to action. Reason, they would have said, leads one to recognize a particular action as fitting in a given set of circumstances and therefore to do it. Hume would have none of this. "'Tis not contrary to reason," he provocatively asserted, "to prefer the destruction of the whole world to the scratching of my finger." To show that he was not embracing the view that only egoism is rational, Hume continued: "'Tis not contrary to reason to choose my total ruin, to prevent the least uneasiness of an Indian or person wholly unknown to me." His point was simply that to have these preferences is to have certain desires or feelings; they are not matters of reason at all. The intuitionists might insist that moral and mathematical reasoning are analogous, but this analogy was not helpful. Knowing a truth of geometry need not motivate one to act in any way.

What of Hume's other premise, that morality is essentially practical and that moral judgments must lead to action? This can be denied more easily. One could say that moral judgments merely tell one what is right or wrong. They do not lead to action unless one wants to do what is right. Then Hume's argument would do nothing to undermine the claim that moral judgments are based on reason. But there is a price to pay: the terms *right* and *wrong* lose much of their force. It can no longer be claimed that those who know what is right but do what is wrong are in any way irrational. They are just people who do not happen to have the desire to do what is right. This desire—because it leads to action—must be acknowledged to be based on feeling rather than on reason. Denying that morality is necessarily action-guiding means abandoning the idea, so important to those defending the objectivity of morality, that some courses of action are objectively required of all rational beings.

Hume's forceful presentation of this argument against a rational basis for morality would have been enough to earn him a place in the history of ethics, but it is by no means his only achievement in this field. In *A Treatise of Human Nature* (1739–40), he points, almost as an afterthought, to the fact that writers on morality regularly start by making various observations about human nature or about the existence of a god—all statements of fact about what is the case—and then suddenly switch to statements about what ought or ought not to be done. Hume says that he cannot conceive how this new relationship of "ought" can be deduced from the preceding statements that were related by "is," and he suggests that these authors should explain how this deduction is to be achieved. The point has since been called Hume's Law and taken as proof of the existence of a gulf between facts and values, or between "is" and "ought." This places too much weight on Hume's brief and ironic comment, but there is no doubt that many writers, both before and after Hume, have argued as if values could easily be deduced from facts. They can usually be found to have smuggled values in somewhere. Attention to Hume's Law makes it easy to detect such logically illicit contraband.

Hume's positive account of morality is in keeping with the moral sense school: "The hypothesis which we embrace is plain. It maintains that morality is determined by sentiment. It defines virtue to be whatever mental action or quality gives to a spectator the pleasing sentiment of approbation; and vice the contrary." In other words, Hume takes moral judgments to be based on a feeling. They do not reflect any objective state of the world. Having said that, however, it may still be asked whether this feeling is one that is common to all or one that varies from individual to individual. If Hume gives the former answer, moral judgments retain a kind of objectivity. While they do not reflect anything "out there" in the universe (apart from human feelings), one's judgments may be true or false depending on whether they capture this universal human moral sentiment. If, on the other hand, the feeling varies from one individual to the next, moral judgments become entirely subjective. People's judgments would express their own feelings, and to reject someone else's judgment as wrong would merely be to say that one's own feelings were different.

Hume does not make entirely clear which of these two views he holds; but if he is to avoid breaching his own rule about not deducing an "ought" from an "is," he cannot hold that a moral judgment can follow logically from a description of the feelings that an action gives to a particular group of spectators. From the mere existence of a feeling, one cannot draw the inference that one ought to obey it. For Hume to be consistent on this point—and consistent even with his central argument that moral judgments must move to action—the moral judgment must be based not on the fact that all people, or most people, or even the speaker, have a certain feeling; it must rather be based on the actual experience of the feeling by whoever accepts the judgment. This still leaves it open whether the feeling is common to all or limited to the person accepting the judgment, but it shows that, in either case, the "truth" of a judgment for any individual depends on whether that individual actually has the appropriate feeling. Is this "truth" at all? As will be seen below, contemporary philosophers with views broadly similar to Hume's have suggested that moral judgments have a special kind of meaning not susceptible of truth or falsity in the ordinary way.

RICHARD PRICE AND THOMAS REID

Powerful as they were, Hume's arguments did not end the debate between the moral sense theorists and the intuitionists. They did, however, lead Richard Price, Thomas Reid, and later intuitionists to abandon the idea that moral truths can be established by some process of demonstrative reasoning akin to that used in mathematics. Instead, these proponents of intuitionism took the line that notions of right and wrong are simple, objective ideas that are directly perceived and not further analyzable into anything such as "fitness." Knowledge of these ideas derives not from any moral sense based on feelings but rather from a faculty of reason or of the intellect that is capable of discerning truth. Since Hume, this has been the only plausible form of intuitionism. Yet, Price and Reid failed to explain adequately what the objective moral qualities are and how they are connected to human action.

UTILITARIANISM

At this point the argument over whether morality is based on reason or on feelings was temporarily exhausted, and the focus of British ethics shifted from such questions about the nature of morality as a whole to an inquiry into which actions are right and which are wrong. Today, the distinction between these two types of inquiry would be expressed by saying that, whereas the 18th-century debate between intuitionism and the moral sense school dealt with questions of metaethics, 19th-century thinkers became chiefly concerned with questions of normative ethics. Metaethical positions concerning whether ethics is objective or subjective, for example, do not tell one what one ought to do. That task is the province of normative ethics.

William Paley

The impetus to the discussion of normative ethics was provided by the challenge of utilitarianism. The essential principle of utilitarianism was put forth by Hutcheson. Curiously, it was further developed by the widely read theologian William Paley, who provides a good example of the independence of metaethics and normative ethics. His position on the nature of morality was similar to that of Ockham and Luther—namely, he held that right and wrong are determined by the will of God. Yet, because he believed that God wills the happiness of his creatures, his normative ethics were utilitarian: whatever increases happiness is right; whatever diminishes it is wrong.

Jeremy Bentham

Notwithstanding these predecessors, Jeremy Bentham is properly considered the father of modern utilitarianism. It was he who made the utilitarian principle serve as the basis for a unified and comprehensive ethical system that applies, in theory at least, to every area of life. Never before had a complete, detailed system of ethics been so consistently constructed from a single fundamental ethical principle.

Bentham's ethics began with the proposition that nature has placed human beings under two masters: pleasure and pain. Anything that seems good must be either directly pleasurable or thought to be a means to pleasure or to the avoidance of pain. Conversely, anything that seems bad must be either directly painful or thought to be a means to pain or to the deprivation of pleasure. From this Bentham argued that the words *right* and *wrong* can be meaningful only if they are used in accordance with the utilitarian principle, so that whatever increases the net surplus of pleasure over pain is right and whatever decreases it is wrong.

Bentham then considered how one is to weigh the consequences of an action and thereby decide whether it is right or wrong. One must, he says, take account of the pleasures and pains of everyone affected by the action, and this is to be done on an equal basis: "Each to count for one, and none for more than one." (At a time when Britain had a major trade in slaves, this was a radical suggestion; and Bentham went farther still, explicitly extending consideration to nonhuman animals.) One must also consider how certain or uncertain the pleasures and pains are, their intensity, how long they last, and whether they tend to give rise to further feelings of the same or of the opposite kind.

Bentham did not allow for distinctions in the quality of pleasure or pain as such. Referring to a popular game, he affirmed that "quantity of pleasure being equal, pushpin is as good as poetry." This led his opponents to characterize his philosophy as one fit for pigs. The charge is only half true. Bentham could have defended a taste for poetry on the grounds that, whereas one tires of mere games, the pleasures of a true appreciation of poetry have no limit; thus, the quantities of pleasure obtained by poetry are greater than those obtained by pushpin. All the same, one of the strengths of Bentham's position is its honest bluntness, which it owes to his refusal to be fazed by the contrary opinions either of conventional morality or of refined society. He never thought that the aim of utilitarianism was to explain or to justify ordinary moral views—it was, rather, to reform them.

JOHN STUART MILL

John Stuart Mill, Bentham's successor as the leader of the utilitarians and the most influential British thinker of the 19th century, had some sympathy for the view that Bentham's position was too narrow and crude. His essay "Utilitarianism" (1861) introduced several modifications, all aimed at a broader view of what is worthwhile in human existence and at implications less shocking to established moral convictions. Although his position was based on the maximization of happiness (and this is said to consist of pleasure and the absence of pain), he distinguished between pleasures that are higher and those that are lower in quality. This enabled him to say that it is "better to be Socrates dissatisfied than a fool satisfied." The fool, he argued, would be of a different opinion only because he has not experienced both kinds of pleasures.

Mill sought to show that utilitarianism is compatible with moral rules and principles relating to justice, honesty, and truthfulness by arguing that utilitarians should not attempt to calculate before each action whether that particular action will maximize utility. Instead, they should be guided by the fact that an action falls under a general principle (such as the principle that people should keep their promises), and adherence to that general principle tends to increase happiness. Only under special circumstances is it necessary to consider whether an exception may have to be made.

HENRY SIDGWICK

Mill's easily readable prose ensured a wide audience for his exposition of utilitarianism, but as a philosopher he was markedly inferior to the last of the 19th-century utilitarians, Henry Sidgwick. Sidgwick's *The Methods of Ethics* (1874) is the most detailed and subtle work of utilitarian ethics yet produced. Especially noteworthy is his discussion of the various principles of what he calls common sense morality—i.e., the morality accepted, without systematic thought, by most people. Price, Reid, and some adherents of their brand of intuitionism thought that such principles (e.g., truthfulness, justice, honesty, benevolence, purity, and gratitude) were self-evident, independent moral truths. Sidgwick was himself an intuitionist as far as the basis of ethics was concerned: he believed that the principle of utilitarianism must ultimately be based on a self-evident axiom of rational benevolence. Nonetheless, he strongly rejected the view that all principles of common sense morality are self-evident. He went on to demonstrate that the allegedly self-evident principles conflict with one another and are vague in their application. They could be part of a coherent system of morality, he argued, only if they were regarded as subordinate to the utilitarian principle, which defined their application and resolved the conflicts between them.

Sidgwick was satisfied that he had reconciled common sense morality and utilitarianism by showing that whatever was sound in the former could be accounted for by the latter. He was, however, troubled by his inability to achieve any such reconciliation between utilitarianism and egoism, the third method of ethical reasoning dealt with in his book. True, Sidgwick regarded it as self-evident that "from the point of view of the universe" one's own good is of no greater value than the like good of any other person, but what could be said to the egoist who expresses no concern for the point of view of the universe, taking his stand instead on the fact that his own good mattered more to him than anyone else's? Bentham had apparently believed either that self-interest and the general happiness are not at odds or that it is the legislator's task to reward or punish actions so as to see that they are not. Mill also had written of the need for sanctions but was more concerned with the role of education in shaping human nature in such a way that one finds happiness in doing what benefits all. By contrast, Sidgwick was convinced that this could lead at best to a partial overlap between what is in one's own interest and what is in the interests of all. Hence, he searched for arguments with which to convince the egoist of the rationality of universal benevolence but failed to find any. *The Methods of Ethics* concludes with an honest admission of this failure and an expression of dismay at the fact that, as a result, "it would seem necessary to abandon the idea of rationalizing [morality] completely."

CHAPTER 5

THE 17TH TO THE 19TH CENTURY: THE EUROPEAN CONTINENT

The major contributors to ethical thought in continental Europe during the modern period were Benedict de Spinoza (1632–77), Jean-Jacques Rousseau (1712–78), Immanuel Kant (1724–1804), Georg Wilhelm Friedrich Hegel (1770–1831), Karl Marx (1818–83), and Friedrich Nietzsche (1844–1900). Although he did relatively little work in ethics, Gottfried Wilhelm Leibniz (1646–1716) is also recognized for his consistent, though implausible, solution to the problem of evil—the problem of reconciling the existence of a God who is all-powerful and perfectly good with the reality of evil in the world.

BENEDICT DE SPINOZA

If Hobbes is to be regarded as the first of a distinctively British philosophical tradition, Benedict de Spinoza, a Dutch-Jewish philosopher, appropriately occupies the same position in continental Europe. Unlike Hobbes, however, Spinoza did not provoke a long-running philosophical debate. In fact, his philosophy was neglected for a century after his death and was in any case much too self-contained a system to invite debate. Nevertheless, Spinoza held positions

Benedict de Spinoza took positions quite contrary to those of Hobbes that were neglected for a century after his death. Imagno/Hulton Archive/ Getty Images

on crucial issues that sharply contrasted with those taken by Hobbes, and these differences were to grow over the centuries during which British and continental European philosophy followed their own paths.

The first of these contrasts with Hobbes is Spinoza's attitude toward natural desires. Hobbes took self-interested desire for pleasure as an unchangeable fact about human nature and proceeded to build a moral and political system to cope with it. Spinoza did just the opposite. He saw natural desires as a form of bondage. One does not choose to have them of his own will. One's will cannot be free if it is subject to forces outside itself. Thus, one's real interest lies not in satisfying these desires but in transforming them by the application of reason. Spinoza thus stands in opposition not only to Hobbes but also to the position later to be taken by Hume, for Spinoza saw reason not as the slave of the passions but as their master.

The second important contrast is that, whereas individual humans and their separate interests are always assumed in Hobbes's philosophy, this separation is simply an illusion from Spinoza's viewpoint. Everything that exists is part of a single system, which is at the same time nature and God. (One possible interpretation of this is that Spinoza was a pantheist, believing that God exists in every aspect of the world and not apart from it.) Humans too are part of this system and are subject to its rationally necessary laws. Once this is understood, it becomes apparent how irrational it would be to desire that things should be different from the way they are. This means that it is irrational to envy, to hate, and to feel guilt, for these emotions presuppose the possibility of things being different. So one ceases to feel such emotions and finds peace, happiness, and even freedom—in Spinoza's terms the only freedom there can be—in understanding the system of which one is a part.

A view of the world so different from everyday conceptions as that of Spinoza cannot be made to seem remotely plausible when presented in summary form. To many philosophers it remains implausible even when complete. Its value for ethics, however, lies not in its validity as a whole but in the introduction into continental European philosophy of a few key ideas: that one's everyday nature may not be one's true nature; that humans are part of a larger unity; and that freedom is to be found in following reason.

GOTTFRIED WILHELM LEIBNIZ

Gottfried Wilhelm Leibniz, a German philosopher and mathematician, believed that the world is governed by a perfect God and hence must be the "best of all possible worlds." As a result of a hilarious parody in *Candide* (1759), a novel by the French writer Voltaire, this position has achieved a certain notoriety. It is not generally recognized, however, that it does at least provide a consistent solution to the problem of evil, which has baffled Christian thinkers for many centuries. Leibniz's solution to the problem may not be plausible, but there may be no better one if the premises above are allowed to pass unchallenged.

The Problem of Evil

The problem of evil arises for any view that affirms the following three propositions: God is almighty, God is perfectly good, and evil exists. An important statement of the problem was provided by David Hume when he asked: "Is [God] willing to prevent evil, but not able? then is he impotent. Is he able, but not willing? then is he malevolent. Is he both able and willing? whence then is evil?" (*Dialogues Concerning Natural Religion*; 1779).

Since well before Hume's time, the problem has been the basis of a positive argument for atheism: If God exists, then he is omnipotent and perfectly good; a perfectly good being would eliminate evil as far as it could; there is no limit to what an omnipotent being can do; therefore, if God exists, there would be no evil in the world; there is evil in the world; therefore, God does not exist. In this argument and in the problem of evil itself, evil is understood to encompass both moral evil (caused by free human actions) and natural evil (caused by natural phenomena such as disease, earthquakes, and floods).

Most thinkers, however, have found this argument too simple, since it does not recognize cases in which eliminating one evil causes another to arise or in which the existence of a particular evil entails some good state of affairs that morally outweighs it. Moreover, there may be logical limits to what an omnipotent being can or cannot do. Most skeptics, therefore, have taken the reality of evil as evidence that God's existence is unlikely rather than impossible.

A variety of arguments have been offered in response to the problem of evil. One argument, known as the free will defense, claims that evil is caused not by God but by human beings, who must be allowed to choose evil if they are to have free will. This response presupposes that humans are indeed free, and it fails to reckon with natural evil, except insofar as the latter is increased by human factors such as greed or thoughtlessness. Another argument, developed by the English philosopher Richard Swinburne, is that natural evils can be the means of learning and maturing. Natural evils, in other words, can help cultivate virtues such as courage and generosity by forcing humans to confront danger, hardship, and need. Such arguments are commonly supplemented by appeals to belief in a life after death, not just as reward or compensation but as the state in which the point of human suffering and the way in which God brings good out of evil will be made clear.

JEAN-JACQUES ROUSSEAU

It was the French philosopher and writer Jean-Jacques Rousseau who took the next step. His *A Discourse on Inequality* (1755) depicted a state of nature very different from that described by Hobbes as well as from Christian conceptions of original sin. Rousseau's "noble savages" lived isolated, trouble-free lives, supplying their simple wants from the abundance that nature provided and even going to each other's aid in times of need. Only when someone claimed possession of a piece of land did laws have to be introduced, and with them came civilization and all its corrupting influences. This is, of course, a message that resembles one of Spinoza's key points: the human nature that one sees in one's fellow citizens is not the only possibility; somewhere, there is something better. If a way to reach it could be found, it would mean the solution to all ethical and social problems.

Rousseau revealed his route in *The Social Contract* (1762), which called for rule by the "general will." This may sound like democracy, but Rousseau's conception of rule by the general will is very different from the modern idea of democratic government. Today, it is taken for granted that in any society the interests of different citizens will be in conflict, and that, as a result, for every majority that succeeds in having its will implemented there will be a minority that fails to do so. For Rousseau, on the other hand, the general will is not the sum of all the individual wills in the community but the true common will of all the citizens. Even if a person dislikes and opposes a decision carried by the majority, that decision represents the general will, the common will in which he shares. For this to be possible, Rousseau must be assuming that there is some common good in which all human beings share and hence that their true interests coincide. As man passes from the state of nature to civil society, he has to "consult his reason rather than study his inclinations." This is not, however, a sacrifice of his true interest, for in following reason he ceases to be a slave to "physical impulses" and so gains moral freedom.

This leads to a picture of civilized human beings as divided selves. The general will represents the rational will of every member of the community. If an individual opposes the decision of the general will, his opposition must stem from his physical impulses and not from his true, autonomous will. For obvious reasons, this idea was to find favour with autocratic leaders of the French Revolution such as Maximilien Robespierre (1758–94). It also had a much-less-sinister influence on one of the outstanding philosophers of modern times: Immanuel Kant.

IMMANUEL KANT

Interestingly, Immanuel Kant acknowledged that he had despised the ignorant masses until he read Rousseau and came to appreciate the worth that exists in every human being. For other reasons too, Kant is part of the tradition deriving from both Spinoza and Rousseau. Like his predecessors, Kant insisted that actions resulting from desires cannot be free. Freedom is to be found only in rational action. Moreover, whatever is demanded by reason must be demanded of all rational beings; hence, rational action cannot be based on an individual's personal desires but must be action in accordance with something that he can will to be a universal law. This view roughly parallels Rousseau's idea of the general will as that which, as opposed to the individual will, a person shares with the whole community. Kant extended this community to all rational beings.

Kant's most distinctive contribution to ethics was his insistence that one's actions possess moral worth only when one does his duty for its own sake. Kant first introduced this idea as something accepted by the common moral consciousness of human beings and only later tried to show that it is an essential element of any rational morality. Kant's claim that this idea is central to the common moral consciousness expressed, albeit in an explicit and extreme form, a tendency of Judeo-Christian ethics; it also revealed how much Western ethical consciousness had changed since the time of Socrates, Plato, and Aristotle.

Does common moral consciousness really insist that there is no moral worth in any action done for any motive other than duty? Certainly one would be less inclined to praise the person who plunges into the surf to rescue a drowning child if one learned that it was done because he or she expected a handsome reward from the child's wealthy parents. This feeling lies behind Kant's disagreement with all those moral philosophers who argued that one should do what is right because that is the path to happiness, either on earth or in heaven. But Kant went farther than this. He was equally opposed to those who regard benevolent or sympathetic feelings as the basis of morality. Here he may be reflecting the moral consciousness of

Is there moral worth in an action, such as rushing to save a drowning swimmer, if it is done for any reason other than obligation? David McNew/Getty Images

18th-century Protestant Germany, but it appears that even then the moral consciousness of Britain, as reflected in the writings of Shaftesbury, Hutcheson, Butler, and Hume, was very different. The moral consciousness of Western civilization at the beginning of the 21st century also appears to be different from the one Kant was describing.

Kant's ethics is based on his distinction between hypothetical and categorical imperatives. He called any action based on desires a hypothetical imperative, meaning by this that it is a command of reason that applies only if one desires the goal in question. For example, "Be honest, so that people will think well of you!" is an imperative that applies only if one wishes to be thought well of. A similarly hypothetical analysis can be given of the imperatives suggested by, say, Shaftesbury's ethics: "Help those in distress, if you sympathize with their sufferings!" In contrast to such approaches, Kant said that the commands of morality must be categorical imperatives: they must apply to all rational beings, regardless of their wants and feelings. To most philosophers this poses an insuperable problem: a moral law that applied to all rational beings, irrespective of their personal wants and desires, could have no specific goals or aims, because all such aims would have to be based on someone's wants or desires. It took Kant's peculiar genius to seize upon precisely this implication, which to others would have refuted his claims, and to use it to derive the nature of the moral law. Because nothing else but reason is left to determine the content of the moral law, the only form this law can take is the universal principle of reason. Thus, the supreme formal principle of Kant's ethics is: "Act only on that maxim through which you can at the same time will that it should become a universal law."

Kant still faced two major problems. First, he had to explain how one can be moved by reason alone to act in accordance with this supreme moral law; and, second, he had to show that this principle is able to provide practical guidance in one's choices. If one combines Hume's theory that reason is always the slave of the passions with Kant's denial of moral worth to all actions motivated by desires, the outcome would be that no actions can have moral worth. To avoid such moral skepticism, Kant maintained that reason alone can lead to action without the support of desire. Unfortunately, he was unable to explain how this is possible, beyond arguing that it is necessary if the common conception of morality is to make sense. Of course, the fact that the alternative leads to so unpalatable a conclusion may be in itself a powerful incentive to believe that somehow a categorical imperative is possible, but this consideration would not be convincing to anyone not already committed to Kant's view of moral worth. At one point Kant appeared to take a different line. He wrote that the moral law inevitably produces a feeling of reverence or awe. If he meant to say that this feeling then becomes the motivation for obedience, however, he was conceding Hume's point that reason alone is powerless to bring about action. It would also be difficult to accept that anything, even the moral law, can necessarily produce a certain kind of feeling in all rational beings regardless of their psychological constitution. Thus, this approach does not succeed in clarifying Kant's position or rendering it plausible.

Kant gave closer attention to the problem of how his supreme formal principle of morality can provide guidance in concrete situations. One of his examples is as follows. Suppose that a person plans to get some money by promising to pay it back, though he has no intention of keeping his promise. The maxim of such an action might be: "Make false promises when it suits you to do so." Could such a maxim be a universal law? Of course not. The maxim is self-defeating, because if promises were so easily broken, no one would rely on them, and the practice of making promises would cease. For this reason, the moral law would not allow one to carry out such a plan.

Not all situations are so easily decided, however. Another of Kant's examples deals with aiding those in distress. Suppose a person sees someone in distress, whom he could easily help, but refuses to do so. Could such a person will as a universal law the maxim that one should refuse assistance to those in distress? Unlike the case of promising, there is no strict inconsistency in this maxim's being a universal law. Kant, however, says that one cannot will it to be such, because one may someday be in distress oneself, and in that case one would want assistance from others. This type of example is less convincing than the previous one. If the person in question values self-sufficiency so highly that he would rather remain in distress than escape from it through the intervention of another, then Kant's principle would not require him to assist those in distress. In effect, Kant's supreme principle of practical reason can tell one what to do only in those special cases in which willing the maxim of one's action to be a universal law yields a contradiction. Outside this limited range, the moral law that was to apply to all rational beings regardless of their wants and desires cannot provide guidance except by appealing to wants and desires.

Kant does offer alternative formulations of the categorical imperative, one of which appears to provide more substantial guidance than the formulation considered thus far. This formulation is: "So act that you treat humanity in your own person and in the person of everyone else always at the same time as an end and never merely as means." The connection between this formulation and the first one is not entirely clear, but the idea seems to be that, in choosing for oneself, one treats oneself as an end; if, therefore, in accordance with the principle of universal law, one must choose so that all could choose similarly, one must treat everyone else as an end as well. Even if this is valid, however, the application of the principle raises further questions. What is it to treat someone merely as a means? Using a person as a slave is an obvious example; Kant, like Bentham, was making a stand against this kind of inequality while it still flourished as an institution in some parts of the world. But to condemn slavery one needs only to give equal weight to the interests of slaves, as utilitarians such as Bentham explicitly did. One may wonder, then, whether Kant's principle offers any advantage over utilitarianism. Modern Kantians hold that it does, because they interpret it as denying the legitimacy of sacrificing the rights of one human being in order to benefit others.

Immanuel Kant held that it is wrong to treat someone merely as a means and not as an end in himself, as in the case of slavery. Private Collection/The Bridgeman Art Library/Getty Images

One thing that can be said confidently is that Kant was firmly opposed to the utilitarian principle of judging every action by its consequences. His ethics is a deontological. In other words, the rightness of an action, according to Kant, depends not on its consequences but on whether it accords with a moral rule, one that can be willed to be a universal law. In one essay Kant went so far as to say that it would be wrong for a person to tell a lie even to a would-be murderer who came to his house seeking to kill an innocent person hidden inside. This kind of situation illustrates how difficult it is to remain a strict deontologist when principles may clash. Apparently Kant believed that his principle of universal law required that one never tell lies, but it could also be argued that his principle of treating everyone as an end would necessitate doing everything possible to save the life of an innocent person. Another possibility would be to formulate the maxim of the action with sufficient precision to define the circumstances under which it would be permissible to tell lies — e.g., perhaps there could be a universal law that permitted lying to people who intend to commit murder. Kant did not explore such solutions, however.

GEORG WILHELM FRIEDRICH HEGEL

Although Kant's philosophy was profoundly influential, there were several aspects of it that troubled later thinkers. One of these problematic aspects was his conception of human nature as irreconcilably split between reason and emotion. In *Letters on the Aesthetic Education of Man* (1795), the dramatist and literary theorist Friedrich von Schiller (1759–1805) suggested that, whereas this division might apply to modern human beings, it was not the case in ancient Greece, where reason and feeling seem to have been in harmony. (There is, as suggested earlier, some basis for this claim, insofar as the Greek moral consciousness did not make the modern distinction between morality and self-interest.) Schiller's suggestion may have been the spark that led Georg Wilhelm Friedrich Hegel to develop the first philosophical system based on the notion of historical change.

As Hegel presents it, all of history is the progress of mind, or spirit, along a logically necessary path that leads to freedom. Human beings are manifestations of this universal mind, though at first they do not realize it. Freedom cannot be achieved until human beings do realize it and so feel at home in the universe. There are echoes of Spinoza in Hegel's idea of mind as something universal and also in his conception of freedom as based on knowledge. What is original, however, is the way in which all of history is presented as leading to the goal of freedom. Thus, Hegel accepts Schiller's view that for the ancient Greeks, reason and feeling were in harmony, but he sees this as a naive harmony that could exist only as long as the Greeks did not see themselves as free individuals with a conscience independent of the views of the community. For freedom to

Georg Wilhelm Friedrich Hegel advanced the first philosophical system built on the idea of historical change. FPG/Hulton Archive/ Getty Images

develop, it was necessary for this harmony to break down. This occurred as a result of the Reformation, with its insistence on the right of individual conscience. But the rise of individual conscience left human beings divided between conscience and self-interest, between reason and feeling. Many philosophers tried unsuccessfully to bridge this gulf until Kant's insistence on duty for duty's sake made the division an apparently inevitable part of moral life. For Hegel, however, the division can be overcome by a synthesis of the harmonious communal nature of Greek life with the modern freedom of individual conscience.

In *The Philosophy of Right* (1821), Hegel described how this synthesis could be achieved in an organic community. The key to his solution is the recognition that human nature is not fixed but is shaped by the society in which one lives. The organic community would foster those desires by which it would be most benefited. It would imbue its members with the sense that their own identity consists in being a part of the community, so that they would no more think of going off in pursuit of their own private interests than one's left arm would think of going off without the rest of the body. Nor should it be forgotten that such organic relationships are reciprocal: the organic community would no more disregard the interests of its members than an individual would disregard an injury to his or her arm. Harmony would thus prevail, but not the naive harmony of ancient Greece. The citizens of Hegel's organic community do not obey its laws and customs simply because they are there. With the independence of mind characteristic of modern times, they can give their allegiance only to institutions that they recognize as conforming to rational principles. The modern organic state, unlike the ancient Greek city-state, is self-consciously based on principles that are rationally justified.

Hegel provided a new approach to the ancient problem of reconciling morality and self-interest. Whereas others had accepted the problem as part of the inevitable nature of things and looked for ways around it, Hegel looked at it historically, seeing it as a problem only in a certain type of society. Instead of attempting to solve the problem as it had existed up to his time, he contemplated the emergence of a new form of society in which it would disappear. In this way, Hegel claimed to have overcome one great problem that was insoluble for Kant.

Hegel also believed that he had rectified another key weakness in Kant's ethics—namely, the difficulty of giving content to the supreme formal moral principle. In Hegel's organic community, the content of one's moral duty would be determined by one's position in society. One would know that his duty was to be a good parent, a good citizen, a good teacher, merchant, or soldier, as the case might be. This ethics has been characterized as "my station and its duties," after the title of a well-known essay by the British Hegelian F.H. Bradley (1846–1924). It might be thought that this is a limited, conservative conception of what one ought to do, especially when compared with Kant's principle of universal law. Hegel would have replied that because the organic community is based on universally valid principles of reason, it complies with Kant's principle of universal law. Moreover, without the specific content provided by the concrete institutions and practices of a society, Kant's principle would remain an empty formula.

Hegel's philosophy has both a conservative and a radical side. The conservative aspect is reflected in the ethics of "my station and its duties" and even more strongly in the significant resemblance between Hegel's detailed description of the organic society and the actual institutions of the Prussian state in which he lived and taught for the last decade of his life. This resemblance, however, was in no way a necessary implication of Hegel's philosophy as a whole. After Hegel's death, a group of his more radical followers known as the Young Hegelians hailed the manner in which he had demonstrated the need for a new form of society to overcome the separation between self and community, but they scorned the implication that the state in which they were living could be this society. Among them was a young student named Karl Marx.

KARL MARX

Karl Marx was often portrayed by his followers as a scientist rather than a moralist. He did not deal directly with the ethical issues that occupied the philosophers so far discussed. His materialist conception of history is, rather, an attempt to explain all ideas, whether political, religious, or ethical, as the product of the particular economic stage that society has reached. Thus, in feudal societies loyalty and obedience to one's lord were regarded as the chief virtues. In capitalist societies, on the other hand, the need for a mobile labour force and expanding markets ensures that the most important value will be freedom—especially the freedom to sell one's labour. Because Marx regarded ethics as a mere by-product of the economic basis of society, he frequently took a dismissive attitude toward it. Echoing the Sophist Thrasymachus, Marx said that the "ideas of the ruling class are in every epoch the ruling ideas." In *The Communist Manifesto* (1848), written with Friedrich Engels (1820–95), he was even more scornful, insisting that morality, law, and religion are "so many bourgeois prejudices behind which lurk in ambush just as many bourgeois interests."

A sweeping rejection of ethics, however, is difficult to reconcile with the highly moralistic tone of Marx's condemnation of the miseries that the capitalist system

Karl Marx thought that simply identifying the world's wrongs would not achieve anything. Henry Guttman/ Hulton Archive/Getty Images

inflicts upon the working class and with his obvious commitment to hastening the arrival of the communism that will end such inequities. After Marx died, Engels tried to explain this apparent inconsistency by saying that as long as society was divided into classes, morality would serve the interest of the ruling class. A classless society, on the other hand, would be based on a truly human morality that served the interests of all human beings. This does make Marx's position consistent by setting him up as a critic, not of ethics as such but rather of the class-based moralities that would prevail until the communist revolution.

Marx's earlier writings—those produced when he was a Young Hegelian—convey a slightly different, though not incompatible, impression of the place of ethics in his thought. There seems no doubt that the young Marx, like Hegel, regarded human freedom as the ultimate goal. He also held, as did Hegel, that freedom could be realized only in a society in which the dichotomy between private interest and the general interest had disappeared. Under the influence of socialism, however, he formed the view that merely knowing what was wrong with the world would

not achieve anything. Only the abolition of private property could lead to the transformation of human nature
and so bring about the reconciliation of the individual
and the community. Theory, Marx concluded, had gone as
far as it could; even the theoretical problems of ethics, as
illustrated in Kant's division between reason and feeling,
would remain insoluble unless one moved from theory
to practice. This is what Marx meant in the famous thesis that is engraved on his tombstone: "The philosophers
have only interpreted the world, in various ways; the point
is to change it." The goal of changing the world stemmed
from Marx's attempt to overcome one of the central problems of ethics. The means now passed beyond philosophy.

FRIEDRICH NIETZSCHE

Friedrich Nietzsche was a literary and social critic, not a
systematic philosopher. In ethics, the chief target of his
criticism was the Judeo-Christian tradition. He described
Jewish ethics as a "slave morality" based on envy. Christian
ethics, in his opinion, is even worse, because it makes a
virtue of meekness, poverty, and humility and requires
one to turn the other cheek rather than struggle. It is
an ethics of the weak, who hate and fear strength, pride,
and self-affirmation. Such an ethics, Nietzsche asserted,
undermines the human drives that have led to the greatest
and most noble human achievements.

Nietzsche thought that the era of traditional religion
was over. (His paradoxical way of expressing this point,
"God is dead," is perhaps his most widely repeated aph-
orism.) Yet, what was to take religion's place? Nietzsche
adopted Aristotle's concept of greatness of soul, the
un-Christian virtue that included nobility and a justified
pride in one's achievements. He suggested a "reevalu-
ation of all values" that would lead to a new ideal: the

Übermensch, a term usually translated as "superman" and given connotations that suggest that Nietzsche would have approved of fascism and particularly German Nazism (National Socialism). Nietzsche's praise of "the will to power" is taken as further evidence of his proto-Nazi views. This interpretation, however, owes much to Nietzsche's racist sister, who after his death compiled a volume of his unpublished writings, arranging them to make it appear that Nietzsche would have endorsed Nazi ideals. In fact, Nietzsche was almost as contemptuous of pan-German racism and anti-Semitism as he was of the ethics of Judaism and Christianity. What Nietzsche meant by *Übermensch* was a person who could rise above the limitations of ordinary morality, and by "the will to power" it seems that Nietzsche had in mind self-affirmation and not necessarily the use of power to oppress others.

Nevertheless, it must be said that Nietzsche left himself wide open to those who wanted his philosophical imprimatur for their crimes against humanity. His belief in the importance of the *Übermensch* made him talk of ordinary people as "the herd," who did not really matter. In *Beyond Good and Evil* (1886), he wrote with approval of "the distinguished type of morality," according to which "one has duties only toward one's equals; toward beings of a lower rank, toward everything foreign to one, one may act as one sees fit, 'as one's heart dictates'"—in any event, beyond good and evil. The point is that the *Übermensch* is above ordinary moral standards: "The distinguished type of human being feels *himself* as value-determining; he does not need to be ratified; he judges 'that which is harmful to me is harmful as such'; he knows that *he* is the something which gives value to objects; he *creates values*." In this Nietzsche was a forerunner of existentialism rather than of Nazism—but then existentialism, precisely because it gives no basis for choosing other than authenticity, is itself compatible with Nazism.

Nietzsche's position on ethical matters contrasts starkly with that of Sidgwick. Sidgwick believed in objective standards of moral judgment and thought that the subject of ethics had over the centuries made progress toward these standards. He regarded his own work as building carefully on that progress. Nietzsche, on the other hand, wished to sweep away everything since Greek ethics—and not keep much of that either. The superior types would then be free to create their own values as they saw fit.

CHAPTER 6

CONTEMPORARY ETHICS

The history of Western ethics from the time of the Sophists to the end of the 19th century shows three constant themes. First, there is the disagreement about whether ethical judgments are truths about the world or only reflections of the wishes of those who make them. Second, there is the attempt to show, in the face of considerable skepticism, either that it is in one's own interest to do what is good or that, even if it is not necessarily in one's own interest, it is the rational thing to do. And third, there is the debate about the nature of goodness and the standard of right and wrong. Since the beginning of the 20th century these themes have been developed in novel ways, and much attention has also been given to the application of ethics to practical problems.

METAETHICS

Metaethics deals not with the substantive content of ethical theories or moral judgments but rather with questions about their nature, such as the question of whether moral judgments are objective or subjective. Among contemporary philosophers in English-speaking countries, those defending the objectivity of moral judgments have most often been intuitionists or naturalists; those taking a different view have held a variety of different positions, including subjectivism, relativism, emotivism, prescriptivism, expressivism, and projectivism.

G.E. MOORE AND THE NATURALISTIC FALLACY

At first the scene was dominated by the intuitionists, whose leading representative was the English philosopher G.E. Moore (1873–1958). In his *Principia Ethica* (1903), Moore argued against what he called the "naturalistic fallacy" in ethics, by which he meant any attempt to define the word *good* in terms of some natural quality—i.e., a naturally occurring property or state, such as pleasure. (The label "naturalistic fallacy" is not apt, because Moore's argument applied equally well, as he acknowledged, to any attempt to define *good* in terms of something supernatural, such as "what God wills.") The "open-question argument," as it came to be known, was in fact used by Sidgwick and to some extent by the 18th-century intuitionists, but Moore's statement of it somehow caught the imagination of philosophers during the first half of the 20th century. The upshot was that for 30 years after the publication of *Principia Ethica*, intuitionism was the dominant metaethical position in British philosophy.

The aim of the open-question argument is to show that *good* is the name of a simple, unanalyzable quality. The argument itself is simple enough: it consists of taking any proposed definition of *good* and turning it into a question. For instance, if the proposed definition is "*Good* means whatever leads to the greatest happiness of the greatest number," then Moore would ask: "Is whatever leads to the greatest happiness of the greatest number good?" Moore is not concerned with whether the answer is yes or no. His point is that, if the question is at all meaningful—if a negative answer is not plainly self-contradictory—then the definition cannot be correct, for a definition is supposed to preserve the meaning of the term defined. If it does, a question of the type Moore asks would seem absurd to anyone who understands the meaning of the term. Compare, for example, "Do all squares have four equal sides?"

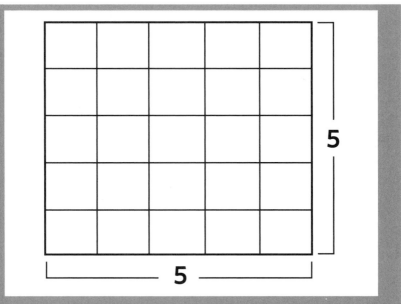

G.E. Moore argued that any question of the form "Is X good?" would seem absurd to anyone who understands the meaning of "good," just as the question of whether all squares have four sides would seem absurd to anyone who understands the concept of the square.

The open-question argument does show that naturalistic definitions do not capture all that is ordinarily meant by the word *good*. It would still be open to a would-be naturalist, however, to argue that, though such naturalistic definitions do not capture all that is ordinarily meant by the word, this does not show that such definitions are wrong; it shows only that the ordinary usage of *good* and related terms is muddled and in need of revision. As to the utilitarian definition of *good* in terms of pleasure, it is questionable whether Mill really intended to offer a definition in the strict sense; he seems instead to have been more interested in offering a criterion by which one could ascertain whether an action was good or bad. As Moore acknowledged, the open-question argument does not show that pleasure, for example, is not the sole criterion of the goodness of an action. It shows only that this fact—if it is a fact—cannot be known merely by inspecting the definition of *good*. If it is known at all, therefore, it must be known by some other means.

Although Moore's antinaturalism was widely accepted by moral philosophers in Britain and other English speaking countries, not everyone was convinced. The American philosopher Ralph Barton Perry (1876–1957), for example, argued (in his *General Theory of Value* [1926]) that there is no such thing as value until a being desires something, and nothing can have intrinsic value considered apart from all desiring beings. A novel, for example, has no value at all unless there is a being who desires to read it or to use it for some other purpose, such as starting a fire on a cold night. Thus, Perry was a naturalist, for he defined value in terms of the natural quality of being desired—or, as he put it, being an "object of an interest." His naturalism is objectivist, despite this dependence of value on desire, because whether an object has value does not depend on the desires of any single individual. Even if one does not desire this novel for any purpose at all, the novel will have some value so long as there is some being who does desire it. Perry believed that it followed from his theory that the greatest value is to be found in whatever leads to the harmonious integration of the desires or interests of all beings.

The open-question argument was taken to show that all attempts to derive ethical conclusions from anything not itself ethical in nature are bound to fail, a point related to Hume's remark about writers who move from "is" to "ought." Moore, however, would have considered Hume's own account of morality to be naturalistic, because it defines virtue in terms of the sentiments of the spectator.

CONTEMPORARY INTUITIONISM

The intuitionists of the 20th century were not philosophically far removed from their 18th-century predecessors, who did not attempt to reason their way to ethical conclusions but claimed rather that ethical knowledge is gained through an immediate apprehension of its truth. According to intuitionists of both eras, a true ethical judgment will be self-evident as long as one is reflecting clearly and calmly and one's judgment is not distorted by self-interest or by faulty moral upbringing. Sir David Ross (1877–1971), for example, took "the convictions of thoughtful, well-educated people" as "the data of ethics," observing that, while some such convictions may be illusory, they should be rejected only when they conflict with others that are better able to stand up to "the test of reflection."

Modern intuitionists differed on the nature of the moral truths that are apprehended in this way. For Moore it was self-evident that certain things are valuable—e.g., the pleasures of friendship and the enjoyment of beauty. Ross, on the other hand, thought that every reflective person knows that he has a duty to do acts of a certain type. These differences will be dealt with in the section on normative ethics. They are, however, significant to metaethical intuitionism because they reveal the lack of agreement, even among intuitionists themselves, about moral judgments that are supposed to be self-evident.

This disagreement was one of the reasons for the eventual rejection of intuitionism, which, when it came, was as complete as its acceptance had been in earlier decades. But there was also a more powerful philosophical motive working against intuitionism. During the 1930s, logical positivism, brought from Vienna by Ludwig Wittgenstein (1889–1951) and popularized by A.J. Ayer (1910–89) in his manifesto *Language, Truth and Logic* (1936), became influential in British philosophy. According to the logical positivists, every true sentence is either a logical truth or a statement of fact. Moral judgments, however, do not fit comfortably into either category. They cannot be logical truths, for these are mere tautologies that convey no more information than what is already contained in the definitions of their terms. Nor can they be statements of fact, because these must, according to the logical positivists, be verifiable (at least in principle); and there is no way of verifying the truths that the intuitionists claimed to apprehend. The truths of mathematics, on which intuitionists had continued to rely as the one clear parallel case of a truth known by its self-evidence, were explained now as logical truths. In this view, mathematics conveys no information about the world; it is simply a logical system whose statements are true by definition. Thus, the intuitionists lost the one useful analogy to which they could appeal in support of the existence of a body of self-evident truths known by reason alone. It seemed to follow that moral judgments could not be truths at all.

EMOTIVISM

In his above-cited *Language, Truth and Logic*, Ayer offered an alternative account: moral judgments are neither logical truths nor statements of fact. They are, instead, merely emotional expressions of one's approval or disapproval of some action or person. As expressions of approval or disapproval, they can be neither true nor false, any more than a tone of reverence (indicating approval) or a tone of abhorrence (indicating disapproval) can be true or false.

This view was more fully developed by the American philosopher Charles Stevenson (1908–79) in *Ethics and Language* (1945). As the titles of the books of this period suggest, moral philosophers (and philosophers in other fields as well) were now paying more attention to language and to the different ways in which it could be used. Stevenson distinguished the facts a sentence may convey from the emotive impact it is intended to have. Moral judgments are significant, he urged, because of their emotive impact. In saying that something is wrong, one is not merely expressing one's disapproval of it, as Ayer suggested. One is also encouraging those to whom he speaks to share his attitude. This is why people bother to argue about their moral views, while on matters of taste they may simply agree to differ. It is important to people that others share their attitudes on moral issues such as abortion, euthanasia, and human rights; they do not care whether others prefer to take their tea with lemon.

The emotivists were immediately accused of being subjectivists. In one sense of the term *subjectivist*, the emotivists could firmly reject this charge. Unlike other subjectivists in the past, they did not hold that those who say, for example, "Stealing is wrong," are making a statement of fact about their own feelings or attitudes toward stealing. This view—more properly known as subjective naturalism because it makes the truth of moral judgments depend on a natural, albeit subjective, fact about the world—could be refuted by Moore's open-question argument. It makes sense to ask: "I know that I have a feeling of approval toward this, but is it good?" It was the emotivists' view, however, that moral judgments make no statements of fact at all. The emotivists could not be defeated by the open-question argument because they agreed that no definition of "good" in terms of facts, natural or unnatural, could capture the emotive element of its meaning. Yet, this reply fails to confront the real misgivings behind the charge of subjectivism: the concern that there are no possible standards of right and wrong other than one's own subjective feelings. In this sense, the emotivists were indeed subjectivists.

EXISTENTIALISM

At about this time a different form of subjectivism was gaining currency on the Continent and to some extent in the United States. Existentialism was as much a literary as a philosophical movement. Its leading figure, the French philosopher Jean-Paul Sartre (1905–80), propounded his ideas in novels and plays as well as in his major philosophical treatise, *Being and Nothingness* (1943). Sartre held that there is no God, and therefore human beings were not designed for any particular purpose. The existentialists expressed this by stating that "existence precedes essence." Thus, they made clear their rejection of the Aristotelian notion that one can know what the good for human beings is once one understands the ultimate end toward which human beings tend. Because humans do not have an ultimate end, they are free to choose how they will live. To say of anyone that he is compelled by his situation, his nature, or his role in life to act in a certain way is to exhibit "bad faith." This seems to be the only term of disapproval the existentialists were prepared to use. As long as a person chooses "authentically," there are no moral standards by which his conduct can be criticized.

This, at least, was the view most widely held by the existentialists. In one work, a pamphlet entitled *Existentialism Is a Humanism* (1946), Sartre backed away from so radical a subjectivism by suggesting a version of Kant's idea that moral judgments be applied universally. He does not reconcile this view with conflicting statements elsewhere in his writings, and it is doubtful whether it represents his final ethical position. It may reflect, however, revelations during the postwar years of atrocities committed by the Nazis at Auschwitz and other death camps. One leading German prewar existentialist, Martin Heidegger (1889–1976), had actually become a Nazi. Was his "authentic choice" to join the Nazi Party just as good as Sartre's own choice to join the French Resistance? Is there really no firm ground from which to compare the two? This seemed to be the outcome of the pure existentialist position, just as it was an implication of the ethical emotivism that was dominant among English-speaking philosophers. It is scarcely surprising that many philosophers should search for a metaethical view that did not commit them to this conclusion. The Kantian avenues pursued by Sartre in *Existentialism Is a Humanism* were also explored in later British moral philosophy, though in a much more sophisticated form.

Universal Prescriptivism

In *The Language of Morals* (1952), the British philosopher R.M. Hare (1919–2002) supported some elements of emotivism but rejected others. He agreed that moral judgments are not primarily descriptions of anything; but neither, he said, are they simply expressions of attitudes. Instead, he suggested that moral judgments are prescriptions—that is, they are a form of imperative sentence, such as, "Save that drowning child!" or "Don't kick that dog!" Hume's rule about not deriving an "is" from an "ought" can best be explained, according to Hare, in terms of the impossibility of deriving any prescription from a set of descriptive sentences. Even the description "There is an enraged bull charging straight toward you" does not necessarily entail the prescription "Run!" because one may have intentionally put oneself in the bull's path as a way of committing suicide. Only the individual can choose whether the prescription fits what he wants. Herein, therefore, lies moral freedom: because the choice of prescription is individual, no one can tell another what is right or wrong.

Hare's espousal of the view that moral judgments are prescriptions led reviewers of his first book to classify him with the emotivists as one who did not believe in the possibility of using reason to arrive at ethical conclusions. That this was a mistake became apparent with the publication of his second book, *Freedom and Reason* (1963). The aim of this work was to show that the moral freedom guaranteed by prescriptivism is, notwithstanding its element of choice, compatible with a substantial amount of reasoning about moral judgments. Such reasoning is possible, Hare wrote, because moral judgments must be "universalizable." This notion owed something to the ancient Golden Rule and even more to Kant's first formulation of the categorical imperative. In Hare's treatment, however, these

From the fact that an angry bull is charging at you, it doesn't follow that you should run. The individual, not the fact, determines what he should do, and herein lies moral freedom, according to R.M. Hare. Three Lions/Hulton Archive/Getty Images

ideas were refined so as to eliminate their obvious defects. Moreover, for Hare universalizability was not a substantive moral principle but a logical feature of moral terms. This means that anyone who uses words such as *right* and *ought* is logically committed to universalizability.

To say that a moral judgment must be universalizable means, for Hare, that anyone who judges a particular action—say, a person's embezzlement of a million dollars from his employer—to be wrong must also judge any relevantly similar action to be wrong. Of course, everything will depend on what is allowed to count as a relevant difference. Hare's view is that all features may count, except those that contain ineliminable uses of words such as *I* or *my* or singular terms such as proper names. In other words, the fact that Smith embezzled a million dollars in order to take holidays in Tahiti whereas Jones embezzled the same sum to give to famine relief in Africa may be a relevant difference; the fact that the first crime benefited Smith whereas the second crime benefited Jones cannot be so.

This notion of universalizability can also be used to test whether a difference that is alleged to be relevant— for instance, skin colour or even the position of a freckle on one's nose—really is relevant. Hare emphasized that the same judgment must be made in all conceivable cases. Thus, if a Nazi were to claim that he may kill a person because that person is Jewish, he must be prepared to prescribe that if, somehow, it should turn out that he is himself of Jewish origin, he should also be killed. Nothing turns on the likelihood of such a discovery; the same prescription has to be made in all hypothetically, as well as actually, similar cases. Since only an unusually fanatic Nazi would be prepared to do this, universalizability is a powerful means of reasoning against certain moral judgments, including those made by Nazis. At the same time, since there could be fanatic Nazis who are prepared to die for the purity of the Aryan race, the argument of *Freedom and Reason* recognizes that the role of reason in ethics does have limits. Hare's position at this stage therefore appeared to be a compromise between the extreme subjectivism of the emotivists and some more objectivist view.

Subsequently, in *Moral Thinking* (1981), Hare argued that to hold an ideal—whether it be a Nazi ideal such as the purity of the Aryan race or a more conventional ideal such as doing justice irrespective of consequences—is really to have a special kind of preference. When asking whether a moral judgment can be prescribed universally, one must take into account all the ideals and preferences held by all those who will be affected by the action one is judging; and in taking these into account, one cannot give any special weight to one's own ideals merely because they are one's own. The effect of this notion of universalizability is that for a moral judgment to be universalizable it must ultimately result in the maximum possible satisfaction of the preferences of all those affected by it. Hare claimed that this reading of the formal property of universalizability inherent in moral language enabled him to solve the ancient problem of showing how moral disagreements can be resolved, at least in principle, by reason. On the other hand, Hare's view seemed to reduce the notion of moral freedom to the freedom to be an amoralist or the freedom to avoid using moral language altogether.

Hare's position was immediately challenged by the Australian philosopher J.L. Mackie (1917–81). In his defense of moral subjectivism, *Ethics: Inventing Right and Wrong* (1977), Mackie argued that Hare had stretched the notion of universalizability far beyond anything inherent in moral language. Moreover, Mackie insisted, even if such a notion were embodied in the ways in which people think and talk about morality, this would not show that the only legitimate moral judgments are those that are universalizable in Hare's sense, because the ways in which people think and talk about morality may be mistaken. Indeed, according to Mackie, the ordinary use of moral language wrongly presupposes that moral judgments are statements about objective features of the world and that they therefore can be true or false. Against this view, Mackie drew upon Hume to argue that moral judgments cannot have the status of matters of fact, because no matter of fact can imply that it is morally right or wrong to act in a particular way (it is impossible, as Hume said, to derive an "ought" from an "is"). If morality is not to be rejected altogether, therefore, it must be allowed that moral judgments are based on individual desires and feelings.

RECENT DEVELOPMENTS IN METAETHICS

Mackie's suggestion that moral language takes a mistakenly realist view of morality effectively ended the preoccupation of moral philosophers with the analysis of the meanings of moral terms. Mackie showed clearly that such an analysis would not reveal whether moral judgments really can be true or false. In subsequent work, moral philosophers tended to keep metaphysical questions separate from semantic ones. Within this new framework, however, the main positions in the earlier debates reemerged, though under new labels. The view that moral judgments can be true or false came to be called "moral realism." Moral realists tended to be either naturalists or intuitionists; they were opposed by "antirealists" or "irrealists," sometimes also called "noncognitivists" because they claimed that moral judgments, not being true or false, are not about anything that can be known. The terminology was sometimes confusing, in particular because moral realism did not imply, as intuitionism and naturalism did earlier, that moral judgments are objective in the sense that they are true or false independently of the feelings or beliefs of the individual.

MORAL REALISM

After the publication of Moore's *Principia Ethica*, naturalism in Britain was given up for dead. The first attempts to revive it were made in the late 1950s by Philippa Foot and Elizabeth Anscombe (1919–2001). In response to Hare's intimation that anything could be a moral principle so long as it satisfied the formal requirement of universalizability in his sense, Foot and Anscombe urged that it was absurd to think that anything so universalizable could be a moral principle; the counterexample they offered was the principle that one should clap one's hands three times an hour. (This principle is universalizable in Hare's sense, because it is possible to hold that all actions relevantly similar to it are right.) They argued that perhaps a moral principle must also have a particular kind of content—that is, it must somehow deal with human well-being, or flourishing. Hare replied that, if "moral" principles are limited to those that maximize well-being, then, for anyone not interested in maximizing well-being, moral principles will have no prescriptive force.

This debate raised the issue of what reasons a person could have for following a moral principle. Anscombe sought an answer to this question in an Aristotelian theory of human flourishing. Such a theory, she thought, would provide an account of what any person must do in order to flourish and so lead to a morality that each person would have a reason to follow (assuming that he had a desire to flourish). It was left to other philosophers to develop such a theory. One attempt, *Natural Law and Natural Rights* (1980), by the legal philosopher John Finnis, was a modern explication of the concept of natural law in terms of a theory of supposedly natural human goods. Although the book was acclaimed by Roman Catholic moral theologians and philosophers, natural law ethics continued to have few followers outside these circles. This school may have been hindered by contemporary psychological theories of human nature, which suggested that violent behaviour, including the killing of other members of the species, is natural in human beings, especially males. Such views tended to cast doubt on attempts to derive moral values from observations of human nature.

As if to make this very point, another form of naturalism arose from a very different set of ideas with the publication of *Sociobiology: The New Synthesis* (1975), by Edward O. Wilson, followed subsequently by the same author's *On Human Nature* (1978) and *Consilience: The Unity of Knowledge* (1999). Wilson, a biologist rather than a philosopher, claimed that new developments in the application of evolutionary theory to social behaviour would allow ethics to be "removed from the hands of philosophers" and "biologicized." He suggested that biology justifies specific moral values, including the survival of the human gene pool and—because humans are mammals rather than social insects—universal human rights.

As the earlier discussion of the origins of ethics suggests, the theory of evolution may indeed reveal something interesting about the origins and nature of the systems of morality used by human societies. Wilson, however, was plainly guilty of breaching Hume's dictum against deriving an "ought" from an "is" when he tried to draw ethical conclusions from scientific premises. Given the premise that human beings wish their species to survive as long as possible, evolutionary theory may indicate some general courses of action that humankind as a whole should pursue or avoid; but even this premise cannot be regarded as unquestionable. For the sake of ensuring a better life, it may be reasonable to run a slight risk that the species

Edward O. Wilson used biology to justify specific moral values, such as universal human rights and the survival of the human gene pool. Steve Liss/ Time & Life Pictures/Getty Images

does not survive indefinitely; it is not even impossible to imagine circumstances in which life becomes so grim that extinction should seem a reasonable choice. Whatever these choices may turn out to be, they cannot be dictated by science alone. It is even less plausible to suppose that the theory of evolution can settle more specific ethical questions. At most, it can indicate what costs humankind might incur by pursuing whatever values it may have.

Very different and philosophically far more sophisticated forms of naturalism were later proposed by several philosophers, including Richard B. Brandt, Michael Smith, and Peter Railton. They held that moral terms are best understood as referring to the desires or preferences that a person would have under certain idealized conditions. Among these conditions are that the person be calm and reflective, that he have complete knowledge of all the relevant facts, and that he vividly appreciate the consequences of his actions for himself and for others. In *A Theory of the Good and the Right* (1979), Brandt went so far as to include in his idealized conditions a requirement that the person be motivated only by "rational desires"— that is, by the desires that he would have after undergoing cognitive psychotherapy (which enables people to understand their desires and to rid themselves of those they do not wish to keep).

Do these forms of naturalism lead to an objectivist view of moral judgments? Consider first Brandt's position. He asked: What rules would a rational person, under idealized conditions, desire to be included in an ideal moral code that all rational people could support? A moral judgment is true, according to Brandt, if it accords with such a code and false if it does not. Yet, it seems possible that different people would desire different rules, even under the idealized conditions Brandt imagined. If this is correct, then Brandt's position is not objectivist, because the standard it recommends for determining the truth or falsity of moral judgments would be different for different people.

In *The Moral Problem* (1994) and subsequent essays, Smith argued that, among the desires that would be retained under idealized conditions, those that deserve the label "moral" must express the values of equal concern and respect for others. Railton, in *Facts, Values and Norms: Essays Toward a Morality of Consequence* (2003), added that such desires must also express the value of impartiality. The practical effect of these requirements was to make the naturalists' ideal moral code very similar to the principles that would be legitimized by Hare's test of universalizability. Again, however, it is unclear whether the idealized conditions under which the code is formulated would be strong enough to lead everyone, no matter what desires he starts from, to endorse the same moral judgments. The issue of whether the naturalists' view is ultimately objectivist or subjectivist depends precisely on the answer to this question.

Another way in which moral realism was defended was by claiming that moral judgments can indeed be true or false, but not in the same sense in which ordinary statements of fact are true or false. Thus, it was argued, even if there are no objective facts about the world to which moral judgments correspond, one may choose to call "true" those judgments that reflect an appropriate "sensibility" to the relevant circumstances. Accordingly, the philosophers who adopted this approach, notably David Wiggins and John McDowell, were sometimes referred to as "sensibility theorists." But it remained unclear what exactly makes a particular sensibility appropriate, and how one would defend such a claim against anyone who judged differently. In the opinion of its critics, sensibility theory made it possible to call moral judgments true or false only at the cost of removing objectivity from the notion of truth—and that, they insisted, was too high a price to pay.

KANTIAN CONSTRUCTIVISM

The most influential work in ethics by an American philosopher in the second half of the 20th century was *A Theory of Justice* (1971), by John Rawls (1921–2002). Although the book was primarily concerned with normative ethics (and so will be discussed in the next section), it made significant contributions to metaethics as well. To argue for his principles of justice, Rawls revived the 17th-century idea of a hypothetical social contract. In Rawls's thought experiment, the contracting parties are placed behind a "veil of ignorance" that prevents them from knowing any particular details about their origins and attributes, including their wealth, their sex, their race, their age, their intelligence, and their talents or skills. Thus, the parties would be discouraged from choosing principles that favour one group at the expense of others, because none of the parties would know whether he belongs to one (or more) of the groups whose interests would thus be neglected. As with the naturalists, the practical effect of this requirement was to make Rawls's principles of justice in many ways similar to those that are universalizable in Hare's sense. As a result of Rawls's work, social contract theory, which had largely been neglected since the time of Rousseau, enjoyed a renewed popularity in ethics in the late 20th century.

Another aspect of Rawls's work that was significant in metaethics was his so-called method of "reflective equilibrium": the idea that the test of a sound ethical theory is that it provide a plausible account of the moral judgments that rational people would endorse upon serious reflection—or at least that it represent the best "balance" between plausibility on the one hand and moral judgments accounted for on the other. In *A Theory of Justice*, Rawls used this method to justify revising the original model of the social contract until it produced results that were not too much at odds with ordinary ideas of justice. To his critics, this move signaled the reemergence of a conservative form of intuitionism, for it meant that the acceptability of an ethical theory would be determined in large part by its agreement with conventional moral opinion.

Rawls addressed the metaethical implications of the method of reflective equilibrium in a later work, *Political Liberalism* (1993), describing it there as "Kantian constructivism." According to Rawls, whereas intuitionism seeks rational insight into true ethical principles, constructivism searches for "reasonable grounds of reaching agreement rooted in our conception of ourselves and in our relation to society." Philosophers do not discover moral truth, they construct it from concepts that they (and other members of society) already have. Because different peoples may conceive of themselves in different ways or be related to their societies in different ways, it is possible for them to reach different reflective equilibria and, on that basis, to construct different principles of justice. In that case, it could not be said that one set of principles is true and another false. The most that could be claimed for the particular principles defended by Rawls is that they offer reasonable grounds of agreement for people in a society such as the one he inhabited.

PROJECTIVISM AND EXPRESSIVISM

The English philosopher Simon Blackburn agreed with Mackie that the realist presuppositions of ordinary moral language are mistaken. In *Spreading the Word* (1985) and *Ruling Passions* (2000), he argued that moral judgments are not statements of fact about the world but a product of one's moral attitudes. Unlike the emotivists, however, he did not regard moral judgments as mere expressions of approval or disapproval. Rather, they are "projections" of people's attitudes onto the world, which are then treated as though they correspond to objective facts. Although moral judgments are thus not about anything really "out there," Blackburn saw no reason to shatter the illusion that they are, for this misconception facilitates the kind of serious, reflective discussion that people need to have about their moral attitudes. (Of course, if Blackburn is correct, then the "fact" that it is good for people to engage in serious, reflective discussion about their moral attitudes is itself merely a projection of Blackburn's attitudes.) Thus, morality, according to Blackburn, is something that can and should be treated as if it were objective, even though it is not.

The American philosopher Alan Gibbard took a similar view of ethics in his *Wise Choices, Apt Feelings* (1990). Although he was an expressivist, holding that moral judgments are expressions of attitude rather than statements of fact, he suggested that thinking of morality as a realm of objective fact helps people to coordinate their behaviour with other members of their group. Because this kind of coordination has survival value, humans have naturally developed the tendency to think and talk of morality in "objectivist" terms. Like Blackburn, Gibbard thought that there is no need to change this way of thinking and talking—and indeed that it would be harmful to do so.

In his last work, *Sorting Out Ethics* (1997), Hare suggested that the debate between realism and irrealism is less important than the question of whether there is such a thing as moral reasoning, about which one can say that it is done well or badly. Indeed, in their answers to this key question, some forms of realism differ more from each other than they do from certain forms of irrealism. But the most important issue, Hare contended, is not so much whether moral judgments express something real about the world but whether people can reason together to decide what they ought to do.

ETHICS AND REASONS FOR ACTION

As noted earlier, Hume argued that moral judgments cannot be the product of reason alone, because they are characterized by a natural inclination to action that reason by itself cannot provide. The view that moral judgments naturally impel one to act in accordance with them—that they are themselves a "motivating reason" for acting—was adopted in the early 20th century by intuitionists such as H.A. Prichard (1871–1947), who insisted that anyone who understood and accepted a moral judgment would naturally be inclined to act on it. This view was opposed by those who believed that the motivation to act on a moral judgment requires an additional, extraneous desire that such action would directly or indirectly satisfy. According to this opposing position, even if a person understands and accepts that a certain course of action is the right thing to do, he may choose to do otherwise if he lacks the necessary desire to do what he believes is right. In the late 20th century, interest in this question enjoyed a revival among moral philosophers, and the two opposing views came to be known as "internalism" and "externalism," respectively.

The ancient debate concerning the compatibility or conflict between morality and self-interest can be seen as a dispute within the externalist camp. Among those who held that an additional desire, external to the moral judgment, is necessary to motivate moral action, there were those who believed that acting morally is in the interest of the individual in the long run and thus that one who acts morally out of self-interest will eventually do well by this standard; others argued that he will inevitably do poorly. Beginning in the second half of the 20th century, this debate was often conducted in terms of the question "Why should I be moral?"

For Hare, the question "Why should I be moral?" amounted to asking why one should act only on those judgments that one is prepared to universalize. His answer was that it may not be possible to give such a reason to a person who does not already want to behave morally. At the same time, Hare believed that the reason why children should be brought up to be moral is that the habits of moral behaviour they thereby acquire make it more likely that they will be happy.

It is possible, of course, to have motivations for acting morally that are not self-interested. One may value benevolence for its own sake, for example, and so desire to act benevolently as often as possible. In that case, the question "Why should I be moral?" would amount to asking whether moral behaviour (whatever it may entail) is the best means of fulfilling one's desire to act benevolently. If it is, then being moral is "rational" for any person who has such a desire (at least according to the conception of reason inherited from Hume—i.e., reason is not a source of moral value but merely a means of realizing the values one already has). Accordingly, in much published discussion of this issue in the late 20th century, the question "Why should I be moral?" was often cast in terms of rationality—i.e., as equivalent to the question "Is it rational to be moral?" (It is important to note that the latter question does not refer to the Humean problem of deriving a moral judgment from reason alone. The problem, on Hume's conception of reason, is rather this: given an individual with a certain set of desires, is behaving morally the best means for him to fulfill those desires?)

In its general form, considered apart from any particular desire, the question "Is it rational to be moral?" is not answerable. Everything depends on the particular desires one is assumed to have. Substantive discussion of the question, therefore, tended to focus on the case of an individual who is fully rational and psychologically normal, and who thus has all the desires such a person could plausibly be assumed to have, including some that are self-interested and others that are altruistic.

Brandt wished to restrict the application of moral terms to the "rational" desires and preferences an individual presumably would be left with after undergoing cognitive psychotherapy. Because such desires would include those that are altruistic, such as the desire to act benevolently and the desire to avoid dishonesty, Brandt's position entails that the moral behaviour by means of which such desires are fulfilled is rational. On the other hand, even a fully rational (i.e., fully analyzed) person, as Brandt himself acknowledged, would have some self-interested desires, and there can be no guarantee that such desires would always be weaker than altruistic desires in cases where the two conflict. Brandt therefore seemed to be committed to the view that it is at least occasionally rational to be immoral.

The American philosopher Thomas Nagel was one of the first contemporary moral philosophers to challenge Hume's thesis that reason alone is incapable of motivating moral action. In *The Possibility of Altruism* (1969), he argued that, if Hume's thesis is true, then the ordinary idea of prudence—i.e., the idea that one's future pains and pleasures are just as capable of motivating one to act (and to act now) as are one's present pains and pleasures—is incoherent. Once one accepts the rationality of prudence, he continued, a very similar line of argument would lead one to accept the rationality of altruism—i.e., the idea that the pains and pleasures of other individuals are just as capable of motivating one to act as are one's own pains and pleasures. This means that reason alone is capable of motivating moral action; hence, it is unnecessary to appeal to self-interest or to benevolent feelings. In later books, including *The View from Nowhere* (1986) and *The Last Word* (1997), Nagel continued to explore these ideas, but he made it clear that he did not support the strong thesis that some reviewers took to be implied by the argument of *The Possibility of Altruism*—that altruism is not merely rational but rationally required. His position was rather that altruism is one among several courses of action open to rational beings. The American philosopher Christine Korsgaard, in *The Sources of Normativity* (1996), tried to defend a stronger view along Kantian lines; she argued that one is logically compelled to regard his own humanity—that is, his freedom to reflect on his desires and to act from reasons—as a source of value, and consistency therefore requires him to regard the humanity of others in the same way. Korsgaard's critics, however, contended that she had failed to overcome the obstacle that prevented Sidgwick from successfully refuting egoism: the objection that the individual's own good provides him with a motivation for action in a way that the good of others does not.

As this brief survey has shown, the issues that divided Plato and the Sophists were still dividing moral philosophers in the late 20th and early 21st century. Ironically, the one position that had few defenders among contemporary philosophers was Plato's view that *good* refers to an idea or property that exists independently of anyone's attitudes, desires, or conception of himself and his relation to society—on this point the Sophists appeared to have won out at last. Yet, there remained ample room for disagreement about whether or in what ways reason can bring about moral judgments. There also remained the dispute about whether moral judgments can be true or false. On the other central question of metaethics, the relationship between morality and self-interest, a complete reconciliation between the two continued to prove as elusive as it did for Sidgwick a century before.

NORMATIVE ETHICS

Normative ethics seeks to set norms or standards for conduct. The term is commonly used in reference to the discussion of general theories about what one ought to do, a central part of Western ethics since ancient times. Normative ethics continued to occupy the attention of most moral philosophers during the early years of the 20th century, as Moore defended a form of consequentialism and as intuitionists such as W.D. Ross (1877–1971) advocated an ethics based on mutually independent duties. The rise of logical positivism and emotivism in the 1930s, however, cast the logical status of normative ethics into doubt: was it not simply a matter of what attitudes one had? Nor was the analysis of language, which dominated philosophy in English-speaking countries during the 1950s, any more congenial to normative ethics. If philosophy could do no more than analyze words and concepts, how could it offer guidance about what one ought to do? The subject was therefore largely neglected until the 1960s, when emotivism and linguistic analysis were both in retreat and moral philosophers once again began to think about how individuals ought to live.

A crucial question of normative ethics is whether actions are to be judged right or wrong solely on the basis of their consequences. Traditionally, theories that judge actions by their consequences were called "teleological," and theories that judge actions by whether they accord with a certain rule were called "deontological." Although the latter term continues to be used, the former has been largely replaced by the more straightforward term "consequentialist." The debate between consequentialist and deontological theories has led to the development of a number of rival views in both camps.

VARIETIES OF CONSEQUENTIALISM

The simplest form of consequentialism is classical utilitarianism, which holds that every action is to be judged good or bad according to whether its consequences do more than any alternative action to increase—or, if that is impossible, to minimize any decrease in—the net balance of pleasure over pain in the universe. This view was often called "hedonistic utilitarianism."

The normative position of Moore is an example of a different form of consequentialism. In the final chapters of *Principia Ethica* and also in *Ethics* (1912), Moore argued that the consequences of actions are decisive for their morality, but he did not accept the classical utilitarian view that pleasure and pain are the only consequences that matter. Moore asked his readers to picture a world filled with all possible imaginable beauty but devoid of any being who can experience pleasure or pain. Then the reader is to imagine another world, as ugly as can be but equally lacking in any being who experiences pleasure or pain. Would it not be better, Moore asked, that the beautiful world rather than the ugly world exist? He was clear in his own mind that the answer was affirmative, and he took this as evidence that beauty is good in itself, apart from the pleasure it brings. He also considered friendship and other close personal relationships to have a similar intrinsic value, independent of their pleasantness. Moore thus judged actions by their consequences, but not solely by the amount of pleasure or pain they produced. Such a position was once called "ideal utilitarianism," because it is a form of utilitarianism based on certain ideals. Since the late 20th century, however, it has more frequently been referred to as "pluralistic consequentialism." Consequentialism thus includes, but is not limited to, utilitarianism.

The position of Hare is another example of consequentialism. His interpretation of universalizability led him to the view that for a judgment to be universalizable, it must prescribe what is most in accord with the preferences of all those who would be affected by the action. This form of consequentialism is frequently called "preference utilitarianism" because it attempts to maximize the satisfaction of preferences, just as classical utilitarianism endeavours to maximize pleasure or happiness. Part of the attraction of such a view lies in the way in which it avoids making judgments about what is intrinsically good, finding its content instead in the desires that people, or

According to G.E. Moore, because a world of beauty, but devoid of any sentient being and thus pleasure or pain, is better than a world of ugliness also devoid of any sentient being, beauty is good in itself, apart from the joy it brings. Gyro Photography/amanaimagesRF/Getty Images

sentient beings generally, do have. Another advantage is that it overcomes the objection, which so deeply troubled Mill, that the production of simple, mindless pleasure should be the supreme goal of all human activity. Against these advantages must be put the fact that most preference utilitarians hold that moral judgments should be based not on the desires that people actually have but rather on those that they would have if they were fully informed and thinking clearly. It then becomes essential to discover what people would desire under these conditions; and, because most people most of the time are less than fully informed and clear in their thoughts, the task is not an easy one.

It may also be noted in passing that Hare claimed to derive his version of utilitarianism from the notion of universalizability, which in turn he drew from moral language and moral concepts. Moore, on the other hand, simply found it self-evident that certain things were intrinsically good. Another utilitarian, the Australian philosopher J.J.C. Smart, defended hedonistic utilitarianism by asserting that he took a favourable attitude toward making the surplus of happiness over misery as large as possible. As these differences suggest, consequentialism can be held on the basis of widely differing metaethical views.

Consequentialists may also be separated into those who ask of each individual action whether it will have the best consequences and those who ask this question only of rules or broad principles and then judge individual actions by whether they accord with a good rule or principle. "Rule-consequentialism" developed as a means of making the implications of utilitarianism less shocking to ordinary moral consciousness. (The germ of this approach was contained in Mill's defense of utilitarianism.) There might be occasions, for example, when stealing from one's wealthy employer in order to give to the poor would have good consequences. Yet, surely it would be wrong to do so. The rule-consequentialist solution is to point out that a general rule against stealing is justified on consequentialist grounds, because otherwise there could be no security of property. Once the general rule has been justified, individual acts of stealing can then be condemned whatever their consequences because they violate a justifiable rule.

This move suggests an obvious question, one already raised by the account of Kant's ethics given above: How specific may the rule be? Although a rule prohibiting stealing may have better consequences than no rule at all, would not the best consequences follow from a rule that permitted stealing only in those special cases in which it is clear that stealing will have better consequences than not stealing? But then what would be the difference between "act-consequentialism" and "rule-consequentialism"? In *Forms and Limits of Utilitarianism* (1965), David Lyons argued that if the rule were formulated with sufficient precision to take into account all its causally relevant consequences, rule-utilitarianism would collapse into act-utilitarianism. If rule-utilitarianism is to be maintained as a distinct position, therefore, there must be some restriction on how specific the rule can be so that at least some relevant consequences are not taken into account.

To ignore relevant consequences, however, is to break with the very essence of consequentialism; rule-utilitarianism is therefore not a true form of utilitarianism at all. That, at least, is the view taken by Smart, who derided rule-consequentialism as "rule-worship" and consistently defended act-consequentialism. Of course, when time and circumstances make it awkward to calculate the precise consequences of an action, Smart's act-consequentialist will resort to rough and ready "rules of thumb" for guidance, but these rules of thumb have no independent status apart from their usefulness in predicting likely consequences. If it is ever clear that one will produce better consequences by acting contrary to the rule of thumb, one should do so. If this leads one to do things that are contrary to the rules of conventional morality, then, according to Smart, so much the worse for conventional morality.

In *Moral Thinking*, Hare developed a position that combines elements of both act- and rule-consequentialism. He distinguished two levels of thought about what one ought to do. At the critical level, one may reason about the principles that should govern one's action and consider what would be for the best in a variety of hypothetical cases. The correct answer here, Hare believed, is always that the best action will be the one that has the best consequences. This principle of critical thinking is not, however, well-suited for everyday moral decision making. It requires calculations that are difficult to carry out even under the most ideal circumstances and virtually impossible to carry out properly when one is hurried or when one is liable to be swayed by emotion or self-interest. Everyday moral decisions, therefore, are the proper domain of the intuitive level of moral thought. At this level one does not enter into fine calculations of consequences; instead, one acts according to fundamental moral principles that one has learned and accepted as determining, for practical purposes, whether an act is right or wrong. Just what these moral principles should be is a task for critical thinking. They must be the principles that, when applied intuitively by most people, will produce the best consequences overall, and they must also be sufficiently clear and brief to be made part of the moral education of children. Hare believed that, given the fact that ordinary moral beliefs reflect the experience of many generations, judgments made at the intuitive level will probably not be too different from judgments made by conventional morality. At the same time, Hare's restriction on the complexity of the intuitive principles is fully consequentialist in spirit.

More recent rule-consequentialists, such as Russell Hardin and Brad Hooker, addressed the problem raised by Lyons by urging that moral rules be fashioned so that they could be accepted and followed by most people. Hardin emphasized that most people make moral decisions with imperfect knowledge and rationality, and he used game theory—the abstract study of situations in which the outcome of a decision made by one person depends on the outcome of decisions made by one or more other people—to show that acting on the basis of rules can produce better overall results than always seeking to maximize utility. Hooker proposed that moral rules be designed to have the best consequences if internalized by the overwhelming majority, now and in future generations. In Hooker's theory, the rule-consequentialist agent is motivated not by a desire to maximize the good but by a desire to act in ways that are impartially defensible.

OBJECTIONS TO CONSEQUENTIALISM

Although the idea that one should do what can reasonably be expected to have the best consequences is obviously attractive, consequentialism is open to several objections. One difficulty is that some of the implications of consequentialism clash with settled moral convictions. Consequentialists, it is said, disregard the Kantian principle of treating human beings as ends in themselves. It is also claimed that, because consequentialists must always aim at the good, impartially conceived, they cannot place adequate value on—or even enter into—the most basic human relationships, such as love and friendship, because these relationships require that one be partial to certain other people, preferring their interests to those of strangers. Related to this objection is the claim that consequentialism is too demanding, for it seems to insist that people constantly compare their most innocent activities with other actions they might perform, some of which—such as fighting world poverty—might lead to a greater good, impartially considered. Another objection is that the calculations that consequentialism demands are too complicated to make, especially if—as in many but not all versions of consequentialism—they require one to compare the happiness or preferences of many different people.

Consequentialists defended themselves against these objections in various ways. Some resorted to rule-consequentialism or to a two-level view like Hare's. Others acknowledged that consequentialism is inconsistent with many widely accepted moral convictions but did not regard this fact as a good reason for rejecting the basic position. A hard-line consequentialist, for example, may argue that the inconsistency is less important than it may seem, because the situations in which it would arise are unlikely ever to occur—e.g., the situation in which one may save the lives of several innocent human beings by killing one innocent human being (in order for this example to count against the consequentialist, one must assume that the killing of the innocent person produces no significant negative consequences other than the death itself). As to the objection that consequentialism is too demanding, some consequentialists simply replied that acting morally is not always an easy thing to do. The difficulty of making interpersonal comparisons of utility was generally acknowledged, but it was also noted that the inexact nature of such comparisons does not prevent people from making them every day, as when a group of friends decides which movie they will see together.

PRIMA FACIE DUTIES

In the first third of the 20th century, the chief alternative to utilitarianism was provided by the intuitionists, especially W.D. Ross. Because of this situation, Ross's normative position was often called "intuitionism," though it would be more accurate and less confusing to reserve this term for his metaethical view (which, incidentally, was also held by Sidgwick) and to refer to his normative position by the more descriptive label, an "ethics of prima facie duties."

Ross's normative ethics consisted of a list of duties, each of which is to be given independent weight: fidelity, reparation, gratitude, beneficence, nonmaleficence, and self-improvement. If an act is in accord with one and only one of these duties, it ought to be carried out. Often, of course, an act will be in accord with two or more duties; e.g., one may respect the duty of gratitude by lending money to a person from whom one once received help, or one may respect the duty of beneficence by loaning the money to others, who happen to be in greater need. This is why the duties are, Ross says, "prima facie" rather than absolute; each duty can be overridden if it conflicts with a more stringent duty.

An ethics structured in this manner may match ordinary moral judgments more closely than a consequentialist ethic, but it suffers from two serious drawbacks. First, how can one be sure that just those duties listed by Ross are independent sources of moral obligation? Ross could respond only that if one examines them closely one will find that these, and these alone, are self-evident. But other philosophers, even other intuitionists, have found that what was self-evident to Ross was not self-evident to them. Second, even if Ross's list of independent prima facie moral duties is granted, it is still not clear how one is to decide, in a particular situation, when a less-stringent duty should be overridden by a more stringent one. Here, too, Ross had no better answer than an unsatisfactory appeal to intuition.

JOHN RAWLS'S THEORY OF JUSTICE

When philosophers again began to take an interest in normative ethics in the 1960s, no theory could rival utilitarianism as a plausible and systematic basis for moral judgments in all circumstances. Yet, many philosophers found themselves unable to accept utilitarianism. One common ground for dissatisfaction was that utilitarianism does not offer any principle of justice beyond the basic idea that everyone's happiness—or preferences, depending on the form of utilitarianism—counts equally. Such a principle is quite compatible with sacrificing the welfare of a few to the greater welfare of the many—hence the enthusiastic welcome accorded to Rawls's *A Theory of Justice* when it appeared in 1971. Rawls offered an alternative to utilitarianism that came close to its rival as a systematic theory of what one ought to do; at the same time, it led to conclusions about justice very different from those of the utilitarians.

As noted earlier, Rawls asserted that if people had to choose principles of justice from behind a veil of ignorance that restricted what they could know of their own positions in society, they would not choose principles designed to maximize overall utility, because this goal might be attained by sacrificing the rights and interests of groups that they themselves belong to. Instead, they would safeguard themselves against the worst possible outcome, first, by insisting on the maximum amount of liberty compatible with the same liberty for others, and, second, by requiring that any redistribution of wealth and other social goods is justified only if it improves the position of those who are worst-off. This second principle is known as the "maximin" principle, because it seeks to maximize the welfare of those at the minimum level of society. Such a principle might be thought to lead directly to an insistence on the equal distribution of goods, but Rawls pointed out that, if one accepts certain assumptions about the effect of incentives and the benefits that may flow to all from the productive labours of the most talented members of society, the maximin principle is consistent with a considerable degree of inequality.

In the decade following its appearance, *A Theory of Justice* was subjected to unprecedented scrutiny by moral philosophers throughout the world. Two major questions emerged: Were the two principles of justice soundly derived from the original contract situation? And did the two principles amount, in themselves, to an acceptable theory of justice?

To the first question, the general verdict was negative. Without appealing to specific psychological assumptions about an aversion to risk—and Rawls disclaimed any such assumptions—there was no convincing way in which Rawls could exclude the possibility that the parties to the original contract would choose to maximize average, rather than overall, utility and thus give themselves the best-possible chance of having a high level of welfare. True, each individual making such a choice would have to accept the possibility that he would end up with a very low level of welfare, but that might be a risk worth taking for the sake of a chance at a very high level.

Even if the two principles cannot be validly derived from the original contract, they might be sufficiently attractive to stand on their own. Maximin, in particular, proved to be a popular principle in a variety of disciplines, including welfare economics, a field in which preference utilitarianism had earlier reigned unchallenged. But maximin also had its critics; one of the charges leveled against it was that it could require a society to forgo very great benefits to the vast majority if, for some reason, they would entail some loss, no matter how trivial, to those who are the worst-off.

Rights Theories

Although appeals to rights have been common since the great 18th-century declarations of the rights of man (the American Declaration of Independence [1776] and the French Declaration of the Rights of Man and of the Citizen [1789]), most ethical theorists have treated rights as something that must be derived from more basic ethical principles or else from accepted social and legal practices. However, beginning in the late 20th century, especially in the United States, rights were commonly appealed to as a fundamental moral principle. *Anarchy, State, and Utopia* (1974), by the American philosopher Robert Nozick (1938–2002), is an example of such a rights-based theory, though it is mostly concerned with applications in the political sphere and says very little about other areas of normative ethics. Unlike Rawls, who for all his disagreement with utilitarianism was still a consequentialist of sorts, Nozick was a deontologist. The rights to life, liberty, and legitimately acquired property are absolute, he insists; no act that violates them can be justified, no matter what the circumstances or the consequences. Nozick also held that one has no duty to help those in need, no matter how badly off they may be, provided that their neediness is not one's fault. Thus, governments may appeal to the generosity of the rich, but they may not tax them against their will in order to provide relief for the poor.

The American philosopher Ronald Dworkin argued for a different view in *Taking Rights Seriously* (1977) and subsequent works. Dworkin agreed with Nozick that rights should not be overridden for the sake of improved welfare: rights are, he said, "trumps" over ordinary consequentialist considerations. In Dworkin's theory, however, the rights to equal concern and respect are fundamental, and observing these rights may require one to assist others in need. Accordingly, Dworkin's view obliges the state to intervene in many areas to ensure that rights are respected.

In its emphasis on equal concern and respect, Dworkin's theory was part of a late 20th–century revival of interest in Kant's principle of respect for persons. This principle, like the value of justice, was often said to be ignored by utilitarians. Rawls invoked Kant's principle when setting out the underlying rationale of his theory of justice. The principle, however, suffers from a certain vagueness, and attempts to develop it into something more specific that could serve as the basis of a complete ethical theory have not been wholly successful.

NATURAL LAW ETHICS

During most of the 20th century, most secular moral philosophers considered natural law ethics to be a lifeless medieval relic, preserved only in Roman Catholic schools of moral theology. In the late 20th century the chief proponents of natural law ethics continued to be Roman Catholic, but they began to defend their position with arguments that made no explicit appeal to religious beliefs. Instead, they started from the claim that there are certain basic human goods that should not be acted against in any circumstances. The list of goods offered by John Finnis in *Natural Law and Natural Rights*, for example, included life, knowledge, play, aesthetic experience, friendship, practical reasonableness, and religion. The identification of these goods is a matter of reflection, assisted by the findings of anthropologists. Furthermore, each of the basic goods is regarded as equally fundamental; there is no hierarchy among them.

It would, of course, be possible to hold a consequentialist ethics that identified several basic human goods of equal importance and judged actions by their tendency to produce or maintain these goods. Thus, if life is a good, any action that led to a preventable loss of life would, other things being equal, be wrong. Proponents of natural law ethics, however, rejected this consequentialist approach; they insisted that it is impossible to measure the basic goods against each other. Instead of relying on consequentialist calculations, therefore, natural law ethics assumed an absolute prohibition of any action that aims directly against any basic good. The killing of the innocent, for instance, is always wrong, even in a situation where, somehow, killing one innocent person is the only way to save thousands of innocent people. What is not adequately explained in this rejection of consequentialism is why the life of one innocent person cannot be measured against the lives of a thousand innocent people—assuming that nothing is known about any of the people involved except that they are innocent.

Natural law ethics recognizes a special set of circumstances in which the effect of its absolute prohibitions would be mitigated. This is the situation in which the so-called doctrine of double effect would apply. If a pregnant woman, for example, is found to have a cancerous uterus, the doctrine of double effect allows a doctor to remove it, notwithstanding the fact that such action would kill the fetus. This allowance is made not because the life of the woman is regarded as more valuable than the life of the fetus, but because in removing the uterus the doctor is held not to aim directly at the death of the fetus; instead, its death is an unwanted and indirect side effect of the laudable act of removing a diseased organ. In cases where the only way of saving the woman's life is by directly killing the fetus, the doctrine provides a different answer. Before the development of modern obstetric techniques, for example, the only way of saving a woman whose fetus became lodged during delivery was to crush the fetus's skull. Such a procedure was prohibited by the doctrine of double effect, for in performing it the doctor would be directly killing the fetus. This position was maintained even in cases where the death of the mother would certainly also bring about the death of the fetus. In these cases, the claim was made that the doctor who killed the fetus directly would be guilty of murder, but the deaths from natural causes of the mother and the fetus would not be his doing. The example is significant, because it indicates the lengths to which proponents of natural law ethics were prepared to go in order to preserve the absolute nature of their prohibitions.

VIRTUE ETHICS

In the last two decades of the 20th century, there was a revival of interest in the Aristotelian idea that ethics should be based on a theory of the virtues rather than on a theory of what one ought to do. This revival was influenced by Elizabeth Anscombe and stimulated by Philippa Foot, who in essays republished in *Virtues and Vices* (1978) explored how acting ethically could be in the interest of the virtuous person. The Scottish philosopher Alasdair MacIntyre, in his pessimistic work *After Virtue* (1980), lent further support to virtue ethics by suggesting that what he called "the Enlightenment Project" of giving a rational justification of morality had failed. In his view, the only way out of the resulting moral confusion was to ground morality in a tradition, such as the tradition represented by Aristotle and Aquinas.

Virtue ethics, in the view of its proponents, promised a reconciliation of morality and self-interest. If, for example, generosity is a virtue, then a virtuous person will desire to be generous; and the same will hold for the other virtues. If acting morally is acting as a virtuous human being would act, then virtuous human beings will act morally because that is what they are like, and that is what they want to do. But this point again raised the question of what human nature is really like. If virtue ethicists hope to develop an objective theory of the virtues, one that is valid for all human beings, then they are forced to argue that the virtues are based on a common human nature; but, as was noted previously in the discussion of naturalism in ethics, it is doubtful that human nature can serve as a standard of what one would want to call morally correct or desirable behaviour. If, on the other hand, virtue ethicists wish to base the virtues on a particular ethical tradition, then they are implicitly accepting a form of ethical relativism that would make it impossible to carry on ethical conversations with other traditions or with those who do not accept any tradition at all.

A rather different objection to virtue ethics is that it relies on an idea of the importance of moral character that is unsupported by the available empirical evidence. There is now a large body of psychological research on what leads people to act morally, and it points to the surprising conclusion that often very trivial circumstances have a decisive impact. Whether a person helps a stranger in obvious need, for example, largely depends on whether he is in a hurry and whether he has just found a small piece of change. If character plays less of a role in determining moral behaviour than is commonly supposed, an ethics that emphasizes virtuous character to the exclusion of all else will be on shaky ground.

FEMINIST ETHICS

In work published from the 1980s, feminist philosophers argued that the prevalent topics, interests, and modes of argument in moral philosophy reflect a distinctively male point of view, and they sought to change the practice of the discipline to make it less male-biased in these respects. Their challenge raised questions in metaethics, normative ethics, and applied ethics. The feminist approach received considerable impetus from the publication of *In a Different Voice* (1982), by the American psychologist Carol Gilligan (b. 1936). Gilligan's work was written in response to research by Lawrence Kohlberg, who claimed to have discovered a universal set of stages of moral development through which normal human beings pass as they mature into adulthood. Kohlberg claimed that children and young adults gradually progress toward more abstract and more impartial forms of ethical reasoning, culminating in the recognition of individual rights. As Gilligan pointed out, however, Kohlberg's study did not include females. When Gilligan studied moral development in girls and young women, she found less emphasis on impartiality and rights and more on love and compassion for the individuals with whom her subjects had relationships. Although Gilligan's findings and methodology were criticized, her suggestion that the moral outlook of women is different from that of men led to proposals for a distinctly feminist ethics—an "ethics of care." As developed in works such as *Caring* (1984), by the American feminist philosopher Nel Noddings, this approach held that normative ethics should be based on the idea of caring for those with whom one has a relationship, whether that of parent, child, sibling, lover, spouse, or friend. Caring should take precedence over individual rights and moral rules, and obligations to strangers may be limited or nonexistent. The approach emphasized the particular situation, not abstract moral principles.

Not all feminist moral philosophers accepted this approach. Some regarded the very idea that the moral perspective of women is more emotional and less abstract than that of men as tantamount to accepting patriarchal stereotypes of women's thinking. Others pointed out that, even if there are "feminine" values that women are more likely to hold than men, these values would not necessarily be "feminist" in the sense of advancing the interests of women. Despite these difficulties, feminist approaches led to new ways of thinking in several areas of applied ethics, especially those concerned with professional fields like education and nursing, as well as in areas that male philosophers in applied ethics had tended to neglect, such as the family.

When studying female moral development, Carol Gilligan found more emphasis on love and compassion than impartiality and rights. Paul Hawthorne/ Getty Images

ETHICAL EGOISM

All of the normative theories considered so far have had a universal focus—i.e., the good they seek to achieve, the character traits they seek to develop, or the principles they seek to apply pertain equally to everyone. Ethical egoism departs from this consensus, because it asserts that moral decision making should be guided entirely by self-interest. One great advantage of such a position is that it avoids any possible conflict between self-interest and morality. Another is that it makes moral behaviour by definition rational (on the plausible assumption that it is rational to pursue one's own interests).

Two forms of egoism may be distinguished. The position of the individual egoist may be expressed as: "Everyone should do what is in my interests." This is indeed egoism, but it is incapable of being universalized (because it makes essential reference to a particular individual); thus, it is arguably not an ethical principle at all. Nor, from a practical perspective, is the individual egoist likely to be able to persuade others to follow a course of action that is so obviously designed to benefit only the person who is advocating it.

Universal egoism is expressed in this principle: "Everyone should do what is in his own interests." Unlike the principle of individual egoism, this principle is universalizable. Moreover, many self-interested people may be disposed to accept it, because it appears to justify acting on desires that conventional morality might prevent one from satisfying. Universal egoism is occasionally seized upon by popular writers, including amateur historians, sociologists, and philosophers, who proclaim that it is the obvious answer to all of society's ills; their views are usually accepted by a large segment of the general public. The American writer Ayn Rand is perhaps the best

20th-century example of this type of author. Her version of egoism, as expounded in the novel *Atlas Shrugged* (1957) and in *The Virtue of Selfishness* (1965), a collection of essays, was a rather confusing mixture of appeals to self-interest and suggestions of the great benefits to society that would result from unfettered self-interested behaviour. Underlying this account was the tacit assumption that genuine self-interest cannot be served by lying, stealing, cheating, or other similarly antisocial conduct.

As this example illustrates, what starts out as a defense of universal ethical egoism very often turns into an indirect defense of consequentialism: the claim is that everyone will be better off if each person does what is in his own interest. The ethical egoist is virtually compelled to make this claim, because otherwise there is a paradox in the fact that he advocates ethical egoism at all. Such advocacy would be contrary to the very principle of ethical egoism, unless the egoist stands to benefit from others' becoming ethical egoists. If his interests are such that they would be threatened by others' pursuing their own interests, then he would do better to advocate altruism and to keep his belief in egoism a secret.

Unfortunately for ethical egoism, the claim that everyone will be better off if each person does what is in his own interests is incorrect. This is shown by thought experiments in game theory known as "prisoner's dilemmas," which played an increasingly important role in discussions of ethical theory in the late 20th century. The basic prisoner's dilemma is an imaginary situation in which two prisoners are accused of a crime. If one confesses and the other does not, the prisoner who confesses will be released immediately and the prisoner who does not will be jailed for 20 years. If neither confesses, each will be held for a few months and then released. And if both confess, each will be jailed for 15 years. It is further stipulated that the prisoners cannot communicate with each other. If each of them decides what to do purely on the basis of self-interest, he will realize that it is better for him to confess than not to confess, no matter what the other prisoner does. Paradoxically, when each prisoner acts selfishly— i.e., as an egoist—the result is that both are worse off than they would have been if each had acted cooperatively.

Although the example might seem bizarre, analogous situations occur quite frequently on a larger scale. Consider the dilemma of the commuter. Suppose that each commuter finds his private car a little more convenient than the bus, but when each commuter drives a car, the traffic becomes extremely congested. So everyone is better off in the situation where everyone takes the bus than in the situation where everyone drives a car. Because private cars are somewhat more convenient than buses, however, and because the overall volume of traffic is not appreciably affected by one more car on the road, it is in the interests of each commuter to continue driving. At least on the collective level, therefore, egoism is self-defeating—a conclusion well brought out by the English philosopher Derek Parfit in *Reasons and Persons* (1984).

The fact that ethical egoism is collectively self-defeating does not mean that it is wrong. An ethical egoist might still maintain that it is right for each person to pursue his own interests, even if this would bring about worse consequences for everyone. His position would not be self-contradictory, though it would be "self-effacing," since it would require him to avoid promoting egoism in public and to keep his true ethical beliefs a secret.

APPLIED ETHICS

The most striking development in the study of ethics since the mid-1960s was the growth of interest among philosophers in practical, or applied, ethics—i.e., the application of normative ethical theories to practical problems. This is not, admittedly, a totally new departure. From Plato onward, moral philosophers have concerned themselves with practical questions, including suicide, the exposure of infants, the treatment of women, and the proper behaviour of public officials. Christian philosophers, notably Augustine and Aquinas, examined with great care such matters as when (if ever) a war is just, whether it is ever right to tell a lie, and whether a Christian woman does wrong by committing suicide to save herself from rape. Hobbes had an eminently practical purpose in writing his *Leviathan*, and Hume wrote about the ethics of suicide. The British utilitarians were very much concerned with practical problems; indeed, they considered social reform to be the aim of their philosophy. Thus, Bentham wrote on electoral and prison reform and animal rights, and Mill discussed the power of the state to interfere with the liberty of its citizens, the status of women, capital punishment, and the right of one state to invade another to prevent it from committing atrocities against its own people.

Nevertheless, during the first six decades of the 20th century, moral philosophers largely neglected applied ethics—something that now seems all but incredible, considering the traumatic events through which most of them lived. The most notable exception, Bertrand Russell (1872–1970), seems to have regarded his writings on ethical topics as largely separate from his philosophical work and did not attempt to develop his ethical views in any systematic or rigorous fashion.

The prevailing view of this period was that moral philosophy is quite separate from "moralizing," a task best left to preachers. What was not generally considered was whether moral philosophers could, without merely preaching, make an effective contribution to discussions of practical issues involving difficult ethical questions. The value of such work began to be widely recognized only during the 1960s, when first the U.S. civil rights movement and subsequently the Vietnam War and the growth of student political activism started to draw philosophers into discussions of the ethical issues of equality, justice, war, and civil disobedience.

Applied ethics soon became part of the philosophy curriculum of most universities in many different countries. Here it is not possible to do more than briefly mention some of the major areas of applied ethics and point to the issues that they raise.

EQUALITY

Since much of the early impetus for the 20th-century revival of applied ethics came from the U.S. civil rights movement, topics such as equality, human rights, and justice were prominent from the beginning. The initial focus, especially in the United States, was on racial and sexual equality. Since there was a consensus that outright discrimination against women and members of racial minority groups (notably African Americans) is wrong, the centre of attention soon shifted to "reverse discrimination": is it acceptable to favour women and members of racial minority groups for jobs and enrollment in universities and colleges because they have been discriminated against in the past?

Inequality between the sexes was another early focus of discussion. Does equality here mean ending as far as possible all differences in the sex roles, or could there be equal status for different roles? There was a lively debate—both between feminists and their opponents and, on a different level, between feminists themselves—about what a society without sexual inequality would be like. Feminist philosophers were also involved in debates about abortion and about new methods of reproduction. These topics will be covered separately below.

Until the late 20th century, most philosophical discussions of justice and equality were limited in scope to a single society. Even Rawls's theory of justice, for example, had nothing to say about the distribution of wealth between societies, an issue that could have made acceptance of his maximin principle much more difficult. In the 1990s philosophers began to think about the moral implications of the vast inequality in wealth between the leading industrialized countries and the countries of the developing world, some of which were afflicted with widespread famine and disease. What obligations, if any, do the citizens of affluent countries have to those who are starving? In *Living High and Letting Die: Our Illusion of Innocence* (1996), the American philosopher Peter Unger made a strong case for the view that any person of reasonable means who neglects to send money to organizations that work to reduce global poverty is thereby doing something seriously wrong. The German-born philosopher Thomas Pogge, in *World Poverty and Human Rights: Cosmopolitan Responsibilities and Reforms* (2002), argued that affluent countries are responsible for increasing the poverty of developing countries and thus for causing millions of deaths annually. In one of his late works, *The Law of Peoples* (1999), Rawls himself turned to the relations between societies, though his conclusions were more conservative than those of Unger and Pogge.

Animals

There is one issue related to equality in which philosophers have led, rather than followed, a social movement.

In the early 1970s, a group of young Oxford-based philosophers began to question the assumption that the moral status of nonhuman animals is automatically inferior to that of humans—as well as the conclusion usually drawn from it, that it is morally permissible for humans to use nonhuman animals as food, even in circumstances where they could nourish themselves well and efficiently without doing so. The publication in 1972 of *Animals, Men and Morals: An Inquiry into the Maltreatment of Nonhumans*, edited by Roslind and Stanley Godlovitch and John Harris, was followed three years later by Peter Singer's *Animal Liberation* and then by a flood of articles and books that established the issue as a part of applied ethics. At the same time, these writings provided a philosophical basis for the animal rights movement, which had a considerable effect on attitudes and practices toward animals in many countries.

Most philosophical work on the issue of animal rights advocated radical changes in the ways in which humans treat animals. Some philosophers, however, defended the status quo, or at least something close to it. In *The Animals Issue: Moral Theory in Practice* (1992), the British philosopher Peter Carruthers argued that humans have moral obligations only to those beings who can participate in a hypothetical social contract. The obvious difficulty with such an approach is that it proves too much: if humanity has no obligations to animals, then it also has no obligations to the minority of humans with severe intellectual disabilities or to future generations of humans, since they too cannot reciprocate. Another British philosopher, Roger Scruton, supported both animal welfare and the right of humans to use animals, at least in circumstances that entailed some benefit to the animals in question. Thus, in *Animal Rights and Wrongs* (2000) he supported foxhunting, because it encourages

Roger Scruton supported foxhunting, arguing that although the animals were indeed harmed, the sport encouraged humans to protect the foxes' habitat. Slim Aarons/Hulton Archive/Getty Images

humans to protect the habitat in which foxes live, but condemned modern "factory" farms, because they do not provide even a minimally acceptable life for the animals raised in them.

THE ENVIRONMENT

Environmental issues raise a host of difficult ethical questions, including the ancient question of the nature of intrinsic value. Whereas many philosophers in the past have agreed that human experiences have intrinsic value—and the utilitarians at least have always accepted that the pleasures and pains of nonhuman animals are of some intrinsic significance—this does not show why it is so bad if dodoes become extinct or a rainforest is cut down. Are these things to be regretted only because of the experiences that would be lost to humans or other sentient beings? Or is there more to it than that? From the late 20th century, some philosophers defended the view that trees, rivers, species (considered apart from the individual animals of which they consist), and perhaps even ecological systems as a whole have a value independent of the instrumental value they may have for humans or nonhuman animals. There is, however, no agreement on what the basis for this value should be.

Concern for the environment also raises the question of obligations to future generations. How much do human beings living now owe to those not yet born? For those who hold a social-contract ethics or for the ethical egoist, the answer would seem to be: nothing. Although humans existing in the present can benefit those existing in the future, the latter are unable to reciprocate. Most other ethical theories, however, do give some weight to the interests of future generations. Utilitarians would not think that the fact that members of future generations do not yet exist is any reason for giving less consideration to their interests than to the interests of present generations—provided that one can be certain that future generations will exist and will have interests that will be affected by what one does. In the case of, say, the storage of radioactive wastes or the emission of gases that contribute to climate change, it seems clear that what present generations do will indeed affect the interests of generations to come. Most philosophers agree that these are important moral issues. Climate change in particular has been conceived of as a question of global equity: how much of a scarce resource (the capacity of the atmosphere safely to absorb waste gases produced by human activity) may each country use? Are industrialized countries justified in using far more of this resource, on a per capita basis, than developing countries, considering that the human costs of climate change will fall more heavily on developing countries because they cannot afford the measures needed to mitigate them?

These questions become even more complex when one considers that the size of future generations can be affected by government population policies and by other less-formal attitudes toward population growth and family size. The notion of overpopulation conceals a philosophical issue that was ingeniously explored in Parfit's *Reasons and Persons*. What is optimum population? Is it the population size at which the average level of welfare will be as high as possible? Or is it the size at which the total amount of welfare—the average multiplied by the number of people—is as great as possible? There were decisive objections to the average view, but the total view also had counterintuitive consequences. Much thought was given to finding alternatives that do not create an obligation to bring more people into the world as long as they will be happy, as the total view implies, or happier than average, as the average view implies. But the alternatives suggested had their own difficulties, and the question remained one of the most baffling conundrums in applied ethics.

WAR AND PEACE

The Vietnam War ensured that the possibility of a just war and the legitimacy of conscription and civil disobedience were prominent in early writings in applied ethics. There was considerable support for civil disobedience against unjust aggression and against unjust laws even in a democracy.

With the end of conscription in the United States and of the war itself two years later (1975), philosophers

Just War

Just war is the notion that the resort to armed force is justified under certain conditions but should also be limited in certain ways. Just war is a Western concept and should be distinguished from the Islamic concept of jihad, or holy war, which in Muslim legal theory is the only type of just war.

Rooted in Classical Roman and biblical Hebraic culture and containing both religious and secular elements, just war first coalesced as a coherent body of thought and practice during the Middle Ages. Rationales for war based on Christian ethics can be found in the writings of St. Augustine and especially St. Thomas Aquinas, whose *Summa Theologiae* (1265/66–1273) outlined the justifications for war and discussed the acts it is permissible to commit in wartime. Secular theorists, who included Hugo Grotius, maintained that war is justifiable only if a country faces imminent danger and the use of force is both necessary and proportionate to the threat.

Most scholars agree that, to be considered just, a war must meet several requirements. The four most important conditions are: (1) the war must be declared openly by a proper sovereign authority; (2) the war must have a just cause (e.g., defense of the common good or a response to grave injustice); (3) the warring state must have just intentions (i.e., it must wage the war for justice rather than for self-interest); and (4) the aim of the war must be the establishment of a just peace. Since the end of World War II it has become customary to add three other conditions: (1) there must be a reasonable chance of success; (2) force must be used as a last resort; and (3) the expected benefits of war must outweigh its anticipated costs.

Since the 1860s written rules governing the conduct of war have been implemented, including rules of engagement for national military forces, the Geneva Conventions (1864–1949) and their protocols (1977), and various agreements limiting the means allowable in war. The Hague Convention (1899 and 1907) and the Geneva Conventions—which attempted to regulate, among other things, the treatment of prisoners of war and civilians—established three principles governing conduct during war: (1) targets should include only combatants and legitimate military and industrial complexes; (2) combatants should not use unjust methods or weapons (e.g., torture and genocide); and (3) the force used should be proportionate to the end sought.

turned their attention to the problem of nuclear weapons. One central question was whether the strategy of nuclear deterrence could be morally acceptable, given that it treats civilian populations as potential nuclear targets. In the 1990s the massacres of civilians in the former Yugoslavia and in Rwanda raised the issue in connection with Mill: the right of one or more countries to intervene in the internal affairs of another country solely because it is engaged in crimes against its own citizens. This issue was taken up within discussions of broader questions dealing with human rights, including the question of whether the insistence that all countries respect human rights is an expression of a universal human value or merely a form of Western "cultural imperialism." At the turn of the 21st century, issues related to the justness of war were raised again in response to the proliferation of chemical and biological weapons and the increasing menace of international terrorism. Some thinkers

The U.S.-led invasion of Iraq is often cited in contemporary debates over the requirements of just war, particularly in light of the large number of civilian casualties. Patrick Baz/AFP/Getty Images

argued that these developments had changed the scope and conditions of justly prosecuted wars, while others vehemently disagreed. The U.S.-led invasion of Iraq in 2003, which ostensibly failed to meet some traditional requirements of just wars, became a much-cited example in these debates.

ABORTION, EUTHANASIA, AND THE VALUE OF HUMAN LIFE

A number of ethical questions are concerned with the end-points of the human life span. The question of whether abortion or the use of human embryos as sources of stem cells can be morally justified was exhaustively discussed in popular contexts, where the answer was often taken to depend directly on the answer to the further question: "When does human life begin?" Many philosophers argued that the latter question was the wrong one to ask, since no conclusion of a specifically moral character follows directly from the scientific fact that human life begins at conception or at some other time. A better approach, according to these philosophers, is to ask what it is that makes killing a human being wrong and then to consider whether these characteristics, whatever they might be, apply to the earliest stages of human life. Although there was no generally agreed-upon answer, some philosophers presented surprisingly strong arguments to the effect that not only the embryo and the fetus but even the newborn infant has no right to life. This position was defended by the British philosopher Jonathan Glover in *Causing Death and Saving Lives* (1977) and in more detail by the Canadian-born philosopher Michael Tooley in *Abortion and Infanticide* (1983).

Such views were hotly contested, especially by those who claimed that all human life, irrespective of its characteristics, is sacrosanct. The task for those who defended the sanctity of human life was to explain why human life, no matter what its characteristics, is specially worthy of protection. Explanation could no doubt be provided in terms of traditional Christian doctrines such as that all humans are made in the image of God or that all humans have an immortal soul. In the philosophical debate, however, opponents of abortion and embryo research eschewed religious arguments of this kind, though without finding a convincing secular alternative.

Somewhat similar issues were raised by the practice of euthanasia when it is nonvoluntary, as in the case of severely disabled newborn infants. Voluntary euthanasia, on the other hand, could be defended on the distinct ground that the state should not interfere with the free, informed choices of its citizens in matters that do not cause harm to others. (The same argument was often invoked in defense of the pro-choice position in the abortion controversy. But it was much weaker in this case, because it presupposed what it needed to prove: namely, that the fetus does not count as a person—or at least not as a person to the extent that the pregnant woman does.) Critics of voluntary euthanasia emphasized practical matters such as the difficulty of maintaining adequate safeguards. Their chief objection, however, was that the practice would lead via a "slippery slope" to nonvoluntary euthanasia and eventually to the compulsory involuntary killing of those the state considers socially undesirable. After the Netherlands became the first country to legalize euthanasia in 2001, studies were undertaken to test this claim. To date, no study has shown any evidence of a slippery slope, but the absence of comparable studies in other countries means that the facts remain in dispute.

BIOETHICS

Ethical issues raised by abortion and euthanasia are part of the subject matter of bioethics, which deals with the ethical dimensions of new developments in medicine and the biological sciences. Inherently interdisciplinary in scope, the field benefits from the contributions of professionals outside philosophy, including physicians, lawyers, scientists, and theologians. Since the late 20th century, centres for research in bioethics have been established in many countries, and medical schools have added the discussion of ethical issues in medicine to their curricula. Governments have sought guidance in setting public policy in particularly controversial areas of bioethics by appointing special committees to provide ethical advice.

Several key themes run through the subjects covered by bioethics. One is whether the quality of a human life can be a reason for ending it or for deciding not to take steps to prolong it. Since medical science can now keep alive severely disabled infants who would otherwise die soon after birth, pediatricians are regularly faced with this question. A major controversy erupted in the United States in 1982 when a doctor agreed to follow the wishes of the parents of an infant with Down syndrome by not carrying out the surgery necessary to save the baby's life. The doctor's decision was upheld by the Supreme Court of Indiana, and the baby died before an appeal could be made to the U.S. Supreme Court. The ensuing discussion and the rules subsequently promulgated by the administration of Pres. Ronald Reagan made it less likely that in the United States an infant with Down syndrome would be denied medically feasible lifesaving surgery, but other countries treated such cases differently. Moreover, in virtually every country, including the United States, there were situations in which doctors decided, on quality-of-life grounds, not to sustain the life of an infant with extremely poor prospects.

Even those who defended the doctrine of the sanctity of all human life did not always insist that doctors use extraordinary means to prolong it. But the distinction between ordinary and extraordinary means, like that between acts and omissions, was problematic. Critics asserted that the wishes of the patient or, if these cannot be ascertained, the quality of the patient's life provides a more relevant basis for a decision than the nature of the means to be used.

Another central theme is that of patient autonomy. This issue arose not only in connection with voluntary euthanasia but also in the area of human experimentation. It was generally agreed that patients must give informed consent to any experimental procedures performed on them. But how much information should they be given? The problem was particularly acute in the case of randomized controlled trials, which require that patients agree to courses of treatment that may consist entirely of placebos. When experiments were carried out using human subjects in developing countries, the difficulties and the potential for unethical practices become greater still. In 2000, the World Medical Association, responding to reports of abuses, revised its Declaration of Helsinki, which sets out the ethical principles that should govern medical research involving human subjects.

The allocation of medical resources became a life-and-death issue in the late 1940s, when hospitals in the United States first obtained dialysis machines and had to choose which of their patients suffering from kidney disease would be allowed to use them. Some bioethicists argued that the decision should be made on a "first come, first served" basis, whereas others thought it obvious that younger patients or patients with dependents should be given preference. Although dialysis machines are no longer so scarce, the availability of various other exotic, expensive lifesaving techniques is limited; hence, the search for rational principles of distribution continues. This problem was particularly complicated in the United States, where access to such techniques often depended on the business decisions of private health insurance firms.

Further advances in biology and medicine gave rise to new issues in bioethics, some of which received considerable public attention. In 1978 the birth of the first human being to be conceived outside a human body initiated a debate about the morality of in vitro fertilization. This soon led to questions about the freezing of human embryos and about what should be done with them if the parents should die. Controversies also arose about the practice of surrogate motherhood, in which a woman is impregnated with the sperm of the husband of an infertile couple (or in some cases with an embryo, after in vitro fertilization) and then surrenders the resulting baby, usually performing this service for a fee. Is this different from selling a baby? If so, how? If a woman who has agreed to act as a surrogate mother changes her mind and decides to keep the baby, should she be allowed to do so?

Since the late 1990s, by far the most controversial issue in bioethics has been cloning. The first successful cloning of a mammal, Dolly the sheep, in 1996 conjured up in the public imagination alarming visions of armies of identical human clones, and many legislatures hastened to prohibit the reproductive cloning of human beings. But the public's reaction resulted more from ignorance and distaste than reflection (which the popular news media did little to encourage). Some bioethicists suggested that in a free society there are no good reasons—apart from the risk that a cloned human may suffer from genetic abnormalities—for cloning to be prohibited. Others viewed cloning as a violation of human dignity, because it would mean that human beings could be designed by other humans. This objection was forcefully stated by the bioethicist Leon Kass, who appealed to what he called, in the title of a 1997 essay, "The Wisdom of Repugnance."

In 1996 Dolly the sheep became famous as the first cloned mammal. Some regarded the idea of human cloning as perfectly acceptable, whereas others considered it a desecration of human dignity. Getty Images

The culmination of such advances in techniques for influencing human reproduction will be the mastery of genetic engineering. Already in the late 20th century, some couples in the United States paid substantial sums for eggs from women with outstanding test scores at elite colleges. (Payment for eggs or sperm was illegal in most other countries.) Prenatal testing for genetic defects was also common, especially in older pregnant women, many of whom terminated the pregnancy when a defect was discovered. Some genetic testing can now be done in embryos in vitro, before implantation. As more genetic tests become available—not only for defects but perhaps eventually for robust health, desirable personality traits, attractive physical characteristics, or intellectual abilities that are under strong genetic influence—humanity will face the question posed by the title of Jonathan Glover's probing book *What Sort of People Should There Be?* (1984). Perhaps this will be the most challenging issue for ethics in the 21st century.

SUMMARY AND CONCLUSION

Ethics is the branch of Western philosophy concerned with what is morally good or bad, right or wrong, and just or unjust. Because its subject matter comprises issues fundamental to practical decision-making, the discipline is closely linked with many other fields of inquiry, including anthropology, economics, politics, and sociology. Ethics, nonetheless, remains distinct from such areas of study in that it is occupied not so much with factual knowledge as it is with values—i.e., human conduct as it ought to be, rather than as it actually is.

Ethics is generally divided into three major subdisciplines: metaethics, normative ethics, and applied ethics. Metaethics centres on questions relating to the nature of moral concepts and judgments. Philosophers in metaethics have taken markedly different positions on this matter. Some have held that moral concepts describe natural or supernatural entities in the world. Others, while agreeing that moral concepts are descriptive of such entities, have maintained that the entities are entirely unique in kind. Still others assert that the primary function of moral concepts is to express attitudes or emotions or to prescribe or prohibit. Corresponding views about the logical status of moral judgments have been held by these various philosophers: either the judgments are capable of being true or false and of constituting a kind of knowledge, or they are incapable of such and function rather to express attitudes or to convey condemnation and praise. There also has been much disagreement over whether moral judgments are objective or subjective, absolute or relative.

Normative ethics is primarily concerned with establishing standards or norms for conduct and is commonly associated with general theories about how one ought to live. One of the central questions of modern normative ethics has to do with whether human actions are to be judged right or wrong solely according to their consequences. Traditionally, theories that judge actions by their consequences have been known as teleological, a term that has in large part been supplanted by *consequentialist*. Another class of theories in normative ethics, designated as deontological, judges actions by their conformance to some formal rule or principle (e.g., the ethical system of the philosopher Immanuel Kant).

Perhaps the most striking development in the study of ethics since the mid-20th century was the growing interest among philosophers in applied ethics—i.e., the application of normative theories to practical moral problems. Such moral issues as racial and sexual equality, human rights, animal rights, and justice have become prominent, as have questions about the value of human life raised by controversies over abortion and euthanasia. Related to the latter are the ethical implications of various developments in regard to reproduction, such as in vitro fertilization, sperm banks, genetic engineering, and cloning. This field of applied ethics, known as bioethics, frequently involves the cooperative efforts of philosophers, physicians, scientists, lawyers, and theologians.

Buddhism A religion and philosophy developed from the teachings of the Buddha (Sanskrit: "awakened one"), a teacher who lived in northern India between the mid-6th and the mid-4th centuries BCE. Spreading from India to Central and Southeast Asia, China, Korea, and Japan, Buddhism has played a central role in the spiritual, cultural, and social life of Asia, and during the 20th century it spread to the West.

Confucianism A worldview, a social ethic, a political ideology, a scholarly tradition, and a way of life originating in ancient China. Sometimes viewed as a philosophy and sometimes as a religion, Confucianism may be understood as an all-encompassing way of thinking and living that entails ancestor reverence and a profound human-centred religiousness.

egoism An ethical theory holding that what is good is whatever promotes one's self-interest.

Epicurean A follower of Epicurus, who identified the supreme good with the absence of bodily and mental pain and advocated the limitation of all desire, the practice of virtue, withdrawal from public life, and the cultivation of friendship.

ethics The branch of philosophy that seeks to determine the correct application of moral notions such as good and bad and right and wrong, or a theory of the application or nature of such notions.

existentialism A philosophical movement oriented toward two major themes, the analysis of human existence and the centrality of human choice.

feminism In philosophy, a loosely related set of approaches that emphasizes the role of gender in the formation of traditional philosophical problems and concepts, analyzes the ways in which traditional philosophy reflects and perpetuates bias against women, and defends philosophical concepts and theories that presume women's equality.

Hinduism The oldest of the world's major religions. It evolved from the Vedic religion of ancient India. The major branches of Hinduism are Vaishnavism and Shaivism, each of which includes many different sects.

intuitionism In metaethics, the view that moral statements can immediately be identified as true or false through a kind of rational intuition.

metaethics The subdiscipline of ethics concerned with determining the nature of moral concepts and judgments.

natural law In philosophy, a system of justice held to be common to all humans and derived from nature rather than from the rules of society.

prescriptivism In metaethics, the view that moral judgments are prescriptions and therefore have the logical form of imperatives.

Protestantism One of the three major branches of Christianity, originating in the 16th–century Reformation. The term applies to the beliefs of Christians who do not adhere to Roman Catholicism or Eastern Orthodoxy. A variety of Protestant denominations grew out of the Reformation.

realism In philosophy, any viewpoint that attributes to the objects of human knowledge an existence that is independent of whether they are being perceived or thought about.

Reformation Also known as the Protestant Reformation, the break with Roman Catholicism and the establishment of Protestant churches in the 16th century.

Renaissance Literally "rebirth," the period in European civilization immediately following the Middle Ages and conventionally held to have been characterized by a surge of interest in Classical learning and values.

Socrates A Greek philosopher whose way of life, character, and thought exerted a profound influence on ancient and modern philosophy. Because he wrote nothing, information about his personality and doctrine is derived chiefly from depictions of his conversations and other information in the dialogues of Plato, in the *Memorabilia* of Xenophon, and in various writings of Aristotle.

Stoic A school of philosophy in Greco-Roman antiquity. Inspired by the teaching of Socrates and Diogenes of Sinope, Stoicism was founded at Athens by Zeno of Citium c. 300 BCE and was influential throughout the Greco-Roman world until at least 200 CE. It stressed duty and held that, through reason, humankind can come to regard the universe as governed by fate and, despite appearances, as fundamentally rational. It maintained that, in regulating one's life, one can emulate the calm and order of the universe by learning to accept events with a stern and tranquil mind.

theology The study of the nature of God or gods and the relationship between the human and divine.

virtue ethics An approach to ethics that considers the notion of virtue (often conceived of as excellence) fundamental. Virtue ethics is primarily concerned with traits of character that are essential to human flourishing, not with the enumeration of duties.

BIBLIOGRAPHY

For an introduction to the major theories of ethics, the reader should consult James Rachels, *The Elements of Moral Philosophy*, 4th ed. (2003).

GENERAL HISTORIES OF WESTERN ETHICS

Robert L. Arrington, *Western Ethics: An Historical Introduction* (1998), contains chapters on the major ethical thinkers from Plato onward. Timothy Shanahan and Robin Wang (eds.), *Reason and Insight: Western and Eastern Perspectives on the Pursuit of Moral Wisdom* (1996), offers introductory accounts of the major ethical traditions of both East and West, supplemented by extracts from the key texts.

ANCIENT GREEK AND ROMAN ETHICS

A good introduction to the ethical thought of the period is William J. Prior, *Virtue and Knowledge: An Introduction to Ancient Greek Ethics* (1991).

EARLY AND MEDIEVAL CHRISTIAN ETHICS

Henry Chadwick, *Augustine: A Very Short Introduction* (1986, reissued 2001), is a useful study. John Finnis, *Aquinas: Moral, Political and Legal Theory* (1998), treats the most influential Scholastic writer on ethics.

THE 17TH TO THE 19TH CENTURY: BRITAIN

Selections of the major texts of this period are brought together in D.D. Raphael (ed.), *British Moralists, 1650–1800*, 2 vol. (1969, reissued 1991). C.D. Broad, *Five Types of Ethical Theory* (1930, reissued 2000), includes clear accounts of the ethics of Butler, Hume, and Sidgwick.

The 17th to the 19th Century: The European Continent

Accessible introductory studies on Rousseau, Nietzsche, Hegel, and Marx have been published by Oxford University Press in its *Very Short Introduction* series. On Kant, readers should consult Roger J. Sullivan, *An Introduction to Kant's Ethics* (1994).

Metaethics

The key articles on moral realism, expressivism, projectivism, and other positions in the contemporary debate can be found in Stephen Darwall, Allan Gibbard, and Peter Railton, *Moral Discourse and Practice: Some Philosophical Approaches* (1997).

Normative Ethics

The best short statement of an act-utilitarian position is J.J.C. Smart's contribution to J.J.C. Smart and Bernard Williams, *Utilitarianism: For and Against* (1973, reprinted 1987). H.J. McCloskey, *Meta-Ethics and Normative Ethics* (1969), is a restatement of the ethic of prima facie duties with some modifications. Roslind Hursthouse, *On Virtue Ethics* (1999), is an informative study.

Applied Ethics

Ruth Chadwick (ed.), *Encyclopedia of Applied Ethics*, 4 vol. (1998), is a major reference source. Good anthologies of articles in applied ethics are Lawrence Hinman (ed.), *Contemporary Moral Issues*, 2nd ed. (2000); John Arthur (ed.), *Morality and Moral Controversies*, 6th ed. (2002); and Hugh Lafollette (ed.), *Ethics in Practice*, 2nd ed. (2002).

INDEX